WHAT IN THE WORLD

IS GOD SAYING ABOUT WOMEN?

What in the World is God saying about Women?

Christine Noble

KINGSWAY PUBLICATIONS
EASTBOURNE

Cover design by Drummond and Peggy Chapman

British Library Cataloguing in Publication Data

Noble, Christine
    What in the world is God saying about women?
    1. Society. Role of women—Christian viewpoints
    I. Title
    261.8'3442

ISBN 0-86065-777-9

Printed in Great Britain for
KINGSWAY PUBLICATIONS LTD
1 St Anne's Road, Eastbourne, E Sussex BN21 3UN by
Richard Clay Ltd, Bungay, Suffolk.
Typeset by Nuprint Ltd, Harpenden, Herts AL5 4SE.

Dedicated to
Joan who began it all,
Ruth who typed it all,
John who edited it all.

Contents

Foreword
by
John Noble

On the 1st March, 1958 as Christine and I were leaving our wedding reception, her father shook me warmly by the hand and said 'I'll give you six months!' Looking back I fully appreciate his reasons for making, what I then took to be, a tongue-in-cheek comment. However, he was almost right.

I'm a fairly strong person and I also find it difficult to resist a challenge. It was a forgone conclusion that once I gazed into Christine's twinkling, 'come-and-get-me-if-you-dare' eyes, I was hopelessly trapped. In my immature and unregenerate state I had visions of rendering her helpless with my charm, but she had other ideas. It seemed that, even though we loved one another, we were doomed to fail from the start. However, the two of us and Christine's Dad had left out one very important factor—the Holy Spirit!

He came, introduced us to Jesus and gave us the Bible. Now it seemed the balance shifted in my favour. It was clear that scripture was on the side of the husband and I made full use of everything I felt it had to offer. 'Wife submit' was a fairly constant demand, and I have to admit Christine did her best. She put her hat on and buttoned her lip, relying on other means (known only to women) to achieve her objectives. Now she confesses that whilst honouring me with her lips she became, at least at times, the 'neck that turned the head!'

With the passing of time and not a few difficulties we began to see that there was a little more to Jesus and his word than the initial, superficial view which had been handed on to us by a church whose roots were firmly embedded in the Victorian era. An era where male domination reached new heights of female suppression albeit veiled in conditional chivalry and respect. Even then the cries of the suffragettes began to be heard and William Booth pioneered fearlessly for women.

Nevertheless, as in so many areas of evangelism and social justice sparked by the revival missionary movement of a century or more ago, the church seemed to fall asleep again tired with all that effort. Only recently, challenged afresh by the need to respond and give an answer to worldly humanist and feminist activists, have we Christians picked up the baton once again. Today there's a fresh breeze blowing in the church and God's people are slowly coming back to life.

The two of us have certainly come through some changes in our thinking. Whilst Christine would still recognise the need to submit to me in the context of our marriage and family life, I see that my task, as a husband and father, is to release my family into their full potential in Christ. I am called to follow Jesus and 'lay down my life for my wife as Christ did for the church'. This is much more demanding than simply working through an authority structure, and calls us both to a deeper reliance on the Holy Spirit to reveal the heart of Jesus and the way he lived.

So this book, rather than being a theological work or a definitive statement on the role and ministry of women in the church, is more the outcome of our struggles, experiences and walk with God together. I'm glad to say that we're practising what we're preaching and Christine has gained respect and credibility as a servant of God in her own right. May she be one of a growing number of women who reject the militant spirit of the age but find strength from the Spirit of God to make their mark and stand for the kingdom of God.

I'm sure that this book will play its part and be a help to many, men and women, who are seeking to move forward in this fundamental area. The unity of men and women in the body of Christ is vital to the fulfilling of our task of reaching the world in our generation.

JOHN NOBLE

I

How on Earth Does a Dizzy Brunette Write a Book Anyway?

How on earth do you write a book about anything, I ask myself, least of all about something which means an enormous amount to you personally?

'I've started this book and given up a dozen times already, my excuses ranging from, 'I can't do it,' to, 'No one will understand what I'm on about and will probably end up disliking and misjudging me without even having met me!' What's more, I'm not a writer and I can't spell to save my life. I'm much more at home reading, or even performing what others have written, than actually writing it myself. But the more I rabbit on, the more I realise that I'm fighting a losing battle. In fact all these reactions are typical of most of us women in the face of such a challenge. Furthermore, it does appear that both God and my husband feel I should be writing, and that seems to me like an overwhelming majority. So here goes!

What's the book about? Well, it's about men, women, God and Satan. 'That just about covers the lot,' I hear you saying. Perhaps I should add that it's also about the fears and phobias which stem from our common Enemy, and our dreams and aspirations

13

which spring directly from our heavenly Father. As you read you'll soon discover that I'm a rather black-and-white person, not only in the way I think but also in the way in which I express myself. So I really don't expect all women or all men to be able to identify totally with everything I have to say. My prayer is that this book will encourage many more people to take a good hard look at themselves, their beliefs and their feelings, in the light of two things. First, Satan's hatred of humanity and his desire to hurt, maim and destroy each one of us. Secondly, God's desire for friendship with us through his Son, Jesus. How terribly things seem to have got out of hand and gone astray from God's original plan and intention. He created this wonderful world, the multitude of stars and other planets, in fact the whole universe and all there is, just for us to enjoy with him.

In all of this grandeur and vastness God has a plan for each individual. The Father I know, feel and love, doesn't view me as part of the seething mass of humanity, but as special, different and unique. The same goes for each one of you. There's nobody like you anywhere now, nor has there been at any other time in history. God thinks you are the 'bee's knees'. However, it does obviously follow that Satan must also have a plan, not so clearly detailed perhaps, as he is not concerned with my individuality. He just wants to use me as part of his overall design to establish his throne and rule. As far as he's concerned I'm just another cog on a huge wheel. Anyone would do. In his economy he wants me as a slave without name or even number.

Let's get it straight at the start: we are in a battle zone. Should anyone reading this not believe in God as their Father and Satan as their Enemy, I hope that before we are through, the Holy Spirit will bring this conflict into focus for you. May you truly come to realise and know for sure, that you are not fighting flesh and blood or mere men and women, but the demon powers which, at present, rule the world. Paul writes in Ephesians chapter 6 and verse 12, '...our struggle is not against flesh and blood, but against the rulers, against the authorities, against the powers of this dark world and against the spiritual forces of evil in the heavenly realms.'

In an endeavour to find their place in God's scheme of things, many people, particularly women, look outside the church for answers to their questions. They may turn towards the feminist movement or the equivalent Christian organisation. It is quite understandable when someone is hurting and desperate for answers, that they will go where their ache will receive attention and apparent healing. However, if we are to avoid fragmentation and division, the remedy must come more and more from within the body of the church, and in particular that means you and me.

My personal plea is that we work together, men and women asking God to lighten our darkness in so many, many areas. We cannot continue to ignore the agonising questions and the pain felt by half the body of Christ. We must not imagine that our women can be placated by the same old dogmas and prejudices which have been churned out over the centuries. The Holy Spirit is breaking in on our puny intellect and theories, bringing a fresh understanding of what God's word truly says and of the dignity which Jesus brought to all creation.

It is my intention to major on the damage inflicted on women. But as I wouldn't want anyone to feel left out or feel that I might be just a wee bit biased towards my own sex, I am taking the liberty to express some of my thoughts concerning men as well. Actually, it's impossible to have a proper perspective of the titanic struggle taking place in the heavenly realm, unless you perceive something of God's purpose for men and women. I'll say more of this later, but one thing I would like to underline at this point—and I feel it cannot be stated too often—is that there should not be a battle going on between the sexes. We must not view the dilemma in which many are caught as simply being male chauvinism and feminism. We need to be more aware of our mutual Enemy and become far more aggressive towards him and all his works. If only we men and women could lay down our verbal weaponry and join together in spiritual warfare, we might then begin to see more of the demonic strongholds come crumbling down.

Have you seen those toys which teach a baby to recognise shapes? They have to pop the square-shaped piece into the square-shaped hole, the cross into the cross-shaped one and so on. None of the pieces will go through any hole other than the one for which it was designed. In the church today we are inclined to view the many facets of God's character rather like this baby's game. We each have a mound of shaped pieces and a box with holes in it. Should we discover a piece which doesn't fit through any hole, we discard it as being irrelevant or, worse, an intrusion. In doing this we bring God down to the size of our own personal experience. Perhaps the answer to our difficulty is that we each have a box with holes in it, but no one box has a capacity for holding all the shapes? Put our boxes together and we may well begin to make some progress with the pile of shaped pieces for which, individually, we personally have no place. Our God can only be fully contained in our relationships together as a body with many members.

So, will you join me in taking the plunge? I warn you now that we shall be looking at the subject with feeling and from a more prophetic and intuitive angle, perhaps through a star-shaped hole! You'll have to go elsewhere for your square, in-depth, theological one! Mind you, I trust I'm not completely devoid of biblical understanding, but there are those more capable than I when it comes to explaining the intricacies of Scripture which have tested scholars over the years. You might say that there are plenty of books being written by women on this subject now. I would have to agree that more women are feeling free to express themselves in writing, but sadly most of them seem to fall into one or two categories. Either they are condescendingly offering us a 'tarted up' version of the old view which keeps us firmly in our place, or they provide an option tainted with feminism which leads us into revolt. I want neither of these. I long to see the fulfilment of what Jesus began two thousand years ago when he made it possible for everyone to become the slaves of his love. In my book I hope to steer a course through the extremes of license and subjugation in harmony with the Scripture, and in so doing help women to take their rightful place in God's plan for our generation.

I trust that at times, as you read, you'll feel as I do. Just when I think I have the whole thing sorted out, God says to me, as he did to Moses at the burning bush, 'I will be what I will be.' The Spirit blows where he chooses and God reveals a new side to his nature. Yet again our little boxes are inadequate. We are overwhelmed by the goodness, the greatness and the diversity of our Father. He constantly leaves me breathless in his presence. Doesn't he do that to you too?

2

Women Are a Damaged Sex

I've already said that God has a plan for each individual and that equally the Devil has his plans also. Part of Satan's plan for me and my sex entails slavery to men and slavery to our emotions. This results in a warped idea of the role of fathers and mothers, being prey to depression, an almost overwhelming fear of criticism and a crippling low opinion of ourselves—and that's simply for starters! I've spoken to hundreds, possibly thousands of women on the subject and when they relax and yield to the prompting of the Holy Spirit, two-thirds admit to these feelings. The other one-third are afraid of criticism should they dare to open up. This state of affairs among women has reached epidemic proportions. Let me unpack some of these thoughts a little more.

Slavery of the female sex is as much an historic fact as black slavery. It is our joint feminine heritage. Until just over a hundred years ago women, as a sex, were without rights at every level and I am talking about here in Britain! And, give or take a decade or two, I believe the same held true for the majority of countries in the Western world. Still today, if we look East, we see the terrible bondage women are in. They are simply chattles, counted with the household effects along with the animals, in many places.

However, coming back closer to home, towards the end of the Victorian era came the 'married woman's settlement law'. For the first time a married woman's property was protected for her against her husband. The situation prior to this was quite bleak for a woman. Once married she had no rights to property, money or even her children. Women were frequently married solely for the size of their dowries or inheritance; love rarely entered into this contract. A man chose his wife on the basis of her monetary worth, or her father sold her for her beauty and sexual attractiveness. Once married, a woman was answerable in everything to her husband in exactly the same way that she was previously answerable to her father. Nothing had changed, only the man to whom she was accountable. Even an heiress on marriage handed everything over and became totally dependent on her husband. The reasoning behind this was quite simple: women didn't have strength or brains. They were weak little creatures and were not to be trusted; they needed to be ordered around and treated just like servants.

The lot of unmarriageable women, meaning those without either beauty or money, was indeed desperate. They were unprepared and untrained to survive in a world without either father or husband. They became part of a grey army of dependent relatives who were passed from home to home as companions and unpaid baby-minders. They were often unwanted and lived out their lives in loneliness and fear. This state among women existed in all stratas of society from the highest to the lowest, from the richest to the poorest. Girls all over the world were resigned to being sold by their fathers. Obviously it wasn't spoken of in these terms, and the world of men then, as today, would be horrified by the analogy to slavery. But what else can you possibly call it when a princess might bring an alliance with another nation, or a waif the price of a meal in exchange for her virginity? Is it any wonder that even in our own enlightened times we are still bound as a sex by this background of subjection and abuse?

I must emphasise that this is not in any way an indictment against men. It simply shows how completely our common Enemy has hoodwinked us and caused us, in our blindness, to co-operate with him in his scheme to bring us into bondage and servitude. These attitudes have been perpetuated in our families right through to today. Parents have been involved in acting out this tragedy over and over again, leaving us with a very distorted picture of what exactly a loving mother and father should be. What is worse, because of this awful situation, we bring this corrupted picture into our relationship with God. Now in our eyes our heavenly Father can assume these earthly weaknesses, and we come to expect the same treatment at the hands of God as we have received from our earthly parents.

When we read stories of sexual abuse in our newspapers we are only seeing the tip of an iceberg when it comes to the way many have been conditioned within their own families. Only in the last year or two have we begun to realise how widespread is the mishandling of our children in this way. Mainly small girls, but also some boys, are being introduced into a sexual relationship with, and by, the one person who should be protecting them throughout childhood from the very acts they are being forced to participate in, namely their fathers. Often, if a girl tries to communicate with her mother about what is happening, the response is anger, disbelief and disgust. Frequently, when the truth does come to light the role played by the mother is minimal.

At best it is unbelieving, at worst there is a silent turning of the back, a passive condoning of the father's actions. Not only sexual abuse, but abuse of all kinds can be found in what appears to be normal, well-clothed, well-fed and well-cared for families. Abuse is not confined to the poor and under-privileged but it can be found right across our society.

What scars can be left on a child's personality when she discovers she was born the wrong sex? Mummy and Daddy really wanted a son, so when the child begins to assimilate and understand the situation she compensates by dressing like a boy. Perhaps she takes up hobbies which are alien to her as a person. She might ask for a carpentry set for Christmas when she is really longing for a doll with curly blonde hair; all this to try to gain affection. Finally, the rejection is complete when the very parents she is trying to win, judge her to be unnatural and lacking in femininity. Perhaps you feel that these kinds of stories are gross exaggerations? I can assure you that having listened to the agonised outpourings from many young girls' and women's hearts on this subject, it is no exaggeration. Indeed, it would be difficult to overstate the case as there has been so much damage inflicted in this way.

Abuse is not confined to the physical and sexual realms, it can also be verbal. Words are spoken which have a damaging and devastating effect. A child constantly told that he or she is thick, an idiot or without intelligence, ends up believing what is said and is effectively, even if advertently, cursed by his or her own parents.

The teenager who is blamed for any disturbance or unhappiness within the family may end up convinced that he should never have been born. This same teenager may resort to the extreme of attempting suicide in an effort to put things right. I prayed for a young man who was suicidal and preoccupied with all aspects of hanging. He constantly asked questions about it, ranging from, 'Is it a very painful way to die?' to, 'Is it a just punishment for wrongdoing?' The Lord was able to uncover the Enemy's curse through a word of knowledge. He had been born with the cord wrapped around his neck, and if it hadn't been for the quick action of the midwife, he would have died. This intervention should have been an evidence in his life of God's hand upon him, but somehow the exact opposite was true. Whenever he was naughty or stepped out of line, his mother said, 'The midwife shouldn't have interfered.' Neither the boy nor his mother had been able to identify the source of his problem. When the Lord stepped in they both understood. The curse was broken and a new sense of release and purpose entered their lives as both were set free.

The continual verbal abuse between husband and wife can bring despair to a woman who, because of her low self-opinion, is only too ready to take on any extra guilt and shame. At a social gathering her man may take a cutting remark or comparison, 'Jane uses the same hairdresser as you do. Why does she look so nice?' 'Don't you think that shade of pink is a bit young for you?' 'Why is it that Mary always manages to make food so interesting?' Of course, when the boot is on the other foot and the woman is scathing, it can be equally as devastating and the result for some men is impotency. 'How is it that Jim manages to escape having a paunch?' 'A good head of hair on a man is very attractive!' 'Wasn't his after-shave dreamy?' Always being told when you fall short and rarely when you succeed, brings lassitude, depression and despair, and creates a terrible, never-ending spiral of relational difficulties.

Women frequently find themselves sexually and verbally abused in their place of work. Whether it is in the office, shop, factory, school, hospital or just walking down the street, women find themselves in embarrassing situations. A man will follow a woman into a stockroom, attempting to touch her and sexually arouse her. He will seek to pass her face to face in any confined space or rub up against her in some way or other. Sadly, some women welcome this sort of attention, always teetering on the edge of sexual commitment. For the women who despise it, quitting their job seems to be the only way out. Trying to tackle the problem can bring further accusations by the male. We do need to recognise these things in our society and also examine their effects upon us as Christians. Believe me, we are not immune to the hurts they can cause.

What about other attitudes persisting today, like ''er indoors' from *Minder* and 'She Who Must Be Obeyed' from *Rumpole*? These are just two light-hearted examples from TV, while we have all the various soap operas with their stereotyped women from the sirens to the slatterns. Television women seem to portray mainly extremes, always being either over- or under-dressed, sexed or endowed. They are either highly intelligent and therefore dangerous or filled with low cunning and evil. The picture presented seems to be pretty much the same in any country, with a few variations. The man is always seen as being hoodwinked by this devious and dogmatic female. Take care, brother. She's out to get you, by fair means or foul!

Men don't escape the TV imagery and conditioning. Adverts encourage them to believe that the smell of their cologne has devastating effects upon us females. Men of low morals or violent nature are admired, just because they care about some aspect of law and order, or perhaps love animals, or are good at sport. In today's world, morality is boring and is not the stuff good

stories are made of. Consequently, our kids grow up
with a false idea of what is manly.

One of the reasons why we women have been 'kept in
our place' is because of our unpredictable feelings. That
we are slaves to our emotions, we have to admit, is all
too often true. We have come to a pretty pass in our
generation when women are encouraged to accept as
normal their emotional extremes because, medically
speaking, pre-menstrual tension, post-menstrual tension and also ovulation tension are the most likely
causes. Should a woman's cycle be every twenty-eight
days, it doesn't take much adding up to see that she
can't have many days left in a month which are free
from depression, emotional upset and pain. I cannot for
the life of me see God's hand in this design—only the
fingerprints of the Enemy. Ladies, please don't over-
react at this point. I will develop and expand these
thoughts in a later chapter. Here I am just stirring you
up, or perhaps for some even whetting your appetite, so
that we will come to see how we have been conditioned
to expect and accept damage from every quarter.

How about that common, and in my opinion worst,
tension of them all, post-natal depression? There is
something about this particular condition which makes
me feel very angry and quite sick. It robs a woman of
the enjoyment of her child. Let's think about it for a
moment. There's all the patience required during the
waiting and growing period, the coming to terms with
her changing shape. There's the difficulty of moving,
the loss of waistline which has made bending an almost
impossible action. It sometimes feels to a mother-to-be
that she hasn't been able to see her own toes for a
lifetime. Then there's the fatigue, the swollen feet and
the hospital visits, all of which in various ways have
been a mixture of anxieties and blessings, and these are
just some of the inconveniences. After all this she now

embarks on the hard physical labour entailed in bringing her child into the world.

The phrase 'having a baby' doesn't begin to give you a true picture of all that is demanded from a woman's body at such a time. It really is 'labour' and can make you sweat! Once all the waiting and birth pains are over, you would think that the new mum would then enter into a time of getting to know and appreciate her baby, but for many mothers this is just not the case. Should post-natal depression hit her, all hope of enjoyment comes to an end for anything from a week to a period of years, while a grey fog descends over all her emotions. Have you ever stopped for a moment, as I have, to ask why? Why should women be prey to such affliction right at this moment of greatest achievement? I simply do not accept that in all cases this suffering is inevitable. I consider that often it is a part of the Enemy's activity aimed directly at my sex to keep us from the enjoyment of the good things God has for us.

Should the things I have written so far be even partially true, how could anyone with this sort of history and background take criticism, even in its mildest form? Allow me to set a little scene for you. Picture a dining room, full of warmth and the good smell of food. The family are seated around the table just about to eat their main meal of the day:

Husband: (Chewing extremely vigorously) 'This meat is tough!'

Wife: 'Well I do my best.' (Bursting into tears) 'I cooked it properly!' (Sob, sob) 'I bought it from the best butcher in town.' (Sob, sob) 'I can't get inside the cow to see how tough it is before I buy it, can I?' (She runs from the room, leaving the family confused and in disarray.)

Does this ring a bell? Do you identify with it? The poor husband had only said that the meat was tough, which was actually true. Attempting to chew it had almost broken his jaw. The woman took the criticism personally and in doing so she took direct responsibility for the cow. What made her respond in this way? Reactions like this can occur over almost anything, from hair shampoo to the weather while on holiday. These incidents can leave a residual feeling of frustration among the onlookers, who are usually members of the family. They may feel that Dad is somehow being unfair and blaming Mum for something over which she has no control. In fact he wasn't blaming anyone at all, unless it was that wretched cow.

Criticism in any form can produce inordinate distress in a woman, wounding her inexplicably. In an effort not to cause this pain, family and friends guard what they say and how they say it. In the end this has the opposite effect, leading to further tension, loss of communication and an even greater sense of rejection. The cry which is frequently heard from a woman to her husband, 'You never talk to me,' may simply be the outcome of him trying to ignore the problem, rather than deal with it. Many men feel that they will lose out, whatever they do or say. Confrontation will force arguments which cannot be resolved, and sentiment will produce distrust.

Talking about these things can be extremely painful, and almost invariably a couple will discover that they need outside help. Perhaps assistance will come from a friend or someone in the church who will seek to remain neutral, yet truthful with you both. Should you be unable to identify your area of difficulty, a trustworthy outside reference point from whom you can receive counsel can be a tremendous asset, saving both time and suffering. Whether you're married or single, the likelihood is that you are wrongly affected by criticism. It simply tends to surface in couples more frequently due to the closeness of the relationship. Recognising that there is a problem and that you do react is the first step to healing. You need help, you need discipline and you need prayer. You also need to identify your Enemy and see that he is active in your life, piling damage upon damage, bruise upon bruise, leaving you to do battle with the very ones you love. From this position of understanding you can go on to the offensive and remove the 'footholds' which Satan has in your life, and freedom is on the way!

3

Damaged as Sinners and Damaged as Saints

For the Christian, the past should have no power over the present, yet sadly for many of us the past continues to have a strong hold upon us and the effect of heredity also play its part. We are unaware of their influences in our lives and therefore fail to see the necessity of having them dealt with by the Lord.

Phrases like, 'He has his father's ears,' or, 'She has her mother's hair,' are quite acceptable. In fact it would be difficult to pretend that it was not true, especially when the likeness is obvious and the ears are like jug-handles or the hair an unusual colour of red. We expect these kinds of remarks and put up with them. The same can be said in the area of our health. 'Well, of course, asthma runs in the family!' You don't need to say any more. Haemophilia, eczema and a multitude of illnesses can be found in generation after generation. This saddens us, but we understand and live with the inevitability of such diseases. Somehow all of this is acceptable to us. But we begin to come undone when we enter into the more mysterious and inexplicable areas. Now we are not quite so complacent.

Here, feelings and emotions come into play. Our

thoughts, if not our spoken words, reject the idea that we can inherit these kinds of traits: irrational fears of the dark, butterflies, hospitals or fire to mention only a few which appear with distressing regularity. On the other side of the coin are the positive characteristics which are passed down the family line: the sunny disposition, the gregarious nature, the infectious laugh or the ability to give. The same applies to other intangible things which recur, like divorce, multiple miscarriages, regular premature deaths, foretelling the future, the Midas touch, the green thumb, the healing hands, creativity, ball sense. These and more can also run in families. The more pleasant side of our inherited nature we are happy to embrace without question. The health hazards we either cope with or, where possible with medical help, seek to eliminate. However, with the strongly negative aspects we seem to have a need to shut them away and ignore them. Is it possible that these traits are inherited, or are they merely the outcome from the roulette of life? Are we stuck with them because they're in our genes, or because they're in the hand which life has dealt?

As Christians we can be so naive! Jesus died and rose again to set us free. We believe this with all of our hearts, but the reality often falls short of the goal. Where does this shortfall occur? Well, it can't be in the Lord. Jesus actually said, 'It is finished.' He did it all, he paid the bill, he settled all our outstanding accounts with God. It is over! This is where I believe our naivety comes into play. We forget that we have an Enemy who has, over generations, infiltrated our families, planting weeds and tares in our lives. We need to enter into battle with the Devil in order to root these out. Jesus wants us to get our feet on Satan's head. It's not enough for him that he has already done just that. He wants us to share the victory. This is where the shortfall is.

Failure to recognise this is the block on us entering into freedom. To put it another way, there is a promised land to be gained, but there are giants who occupy the territory which is rightfully ours. We have to acknowledge and identify these giants before we can properly deal with them. We are in a real battle with a real Enemy and there is a real victory to be won. Hallelujah!

All too often, then, an initial encounter with Jesus just does not always sweep all this inherited history away. A start is made. God's Spirit fuses with our spirit to become one. We now have something of God living within us which is pure gold, it is priceless, it is incorruptible, Satan cannot touch it. Unfortunately, we also have a lot of garbage which must be removed. With the Lord's help we can now begin to sort through and throw the unwanted things out. Sadly for women, this liberation which has just begun at conversion falters, slows down and sometimes comes to a complete standstill. This was my own experience. Now some years on I know my own pattern is not at all unique. In fact it is quite usual.

I was born into the family of God during what I call the 'do not era'. You didn't show your emotions too much, you didn't dance, you didn't act, you didn't go to the cinema, you didn't listen to worldly music (unless it was the classics, of course!). No one seemed to have properly thought these issues through. For example, today's classics are yesterday's pop and were often written by debauched people. They were no more sanctified than the Rolling Stones.

Now these 'do nots' covered all areas of activity. At one time, if John and I wanted to celebrate our anniversary the choice was simple. The only 'safe' places for Christians were the Bible study or the prayer meeting. Anything else could have exposed us to sin. So, I met with Jesus and was presented with a Bible in one hand

and a hat in the other. The latter I needed because I was a woman and the former, which I was already beginning to enjoy, now became 'required reading'. In fact it was the only kind of reading allowed. Something within me that had just been born seemed to be in danger of being stifled right at the birth.

At this time I was a teacher. I had finished my course at the Royal Academy of Dramatic Art and had chosen to teach rather than to perform. The book of Christian rules cast grave doubts on my talent—it was questionable. Inside me was this sinking feeling, this sense of being a misfit. I knew it, I just knew it, there was something wrong with me! I had been an aspiring actress, believing in my talent and my ability to use it. I saw myself as an equal to my peers at college and had developed a specific bent towards comedy. I could, and did, play tragedy, but I shone when it came to farce. Now the whole thing was a 'no go' area, another one of those Christian 'thou shalt nots'.

As a young Christian I entered into a new world. Before I had been a happy pagan, albeit a moral one. Then Jesus came into my life to set me free, but at the same time he was supposed to be giving me a list of things I could not do or be. The restrictions were given, not because I was inefficient, not because I had tried and failed or discovered my inability to function, but solely because I was a female. 'There's something wrong with me!' I thought. My first reaction was to ask 'why?'. In fact I think my middle and last reactions were also 'why?'. The answer I was given at that time to my question was, 'That's the way it is in the church.' I was pointed to a few Bible verses which were never properly explained. I pushed down my next 'why?', put my hat on and kept quiet for a while.

I accepted what I was told. I was unsure of myself in what was, for the most part, a male-dominated church and at that time I didn't have much understanding about myself and my sex. The effect of all this was to reinforce the feelings I had imbibed. God was no different from men in the world. I knew that most fathers had a preference for sons; they were strongly biased towards them as mine had been. Now it seemed God preferred them also. Over the top? Maybe not every female would feel this as strongly as I have written, but the majority would be able to identify to a greater or lesser degree.

It wasn't until many years after I became a Christian that God showed me, through a dream, the effect this had had in my own life. In certain situations, with specific people, I had reactions which I neither understood nor could cope with. In particular I was affected in my communication with John, my own husband. Neither of us could understand what happened at these times or what caused the blockage. Then I had the dream. I dreamed I was in a devastated valley. Nothing grew there, not a single blade of grass. The only thing in the valley with me was a black box. The emotion of fear that overwhelmed me when I looked at this box was indescribable. God spoke and told me that this barren valley was my life. If I wanted to see the valley blossom and become verdant I had to open this box myself. You see, I knew that there was something in the box which chose its own time to come out. Now I had to let it out myself. In my dream I was sweating with apprehension, but I threw open the box and covered my face with my hands. A large black bird flew out, and looking through my fingers I saw it had the cruellest beak made of stainless steel. The bird flew about the valley and when it saw a tiny blade of grass, it swooped down upon it, pulling it out roots and all. The bird ate everything. I saw that if this were allowed to continue, all hope of the valley producing life of any kind would disappear. Then

I woke up. I knew that if I wanted to understand my dream and be set free, I had to look into the face of the bird and confront it.

During the day that followed, I struggled. All sorts of emotions chased each other through my heart and mind. How I functioned normally I can only attribute to the grace of God. Finally, I made my decision and going to my bedroom I asked the Lord to be with me while I looked into the face of the bird. When I did so, I saw that it had the face of my father. Something inside of me burst and I had a physical experience of a presence leaving me. I had been delivered from a spirit of panic. I suppose you were expecting me to say it was rejection, or self-doubt, or even fear. All of those things had played a part in my life up to this point, but they were the leaves, flowers and fruit of a hideous, satanic plant, the root of which was panic. During the hour or so after facing my bird, the Lord brought many incidents to my mind and I was, by his grace, able to deal with them and come to a place of peace in him. I was able to forgive my father completely for any part he had played in all this. Feelings of fear, rejection and self-doubt continued to affect me, but I knew they were only surviving just as picked flowers do in a vase, for a limited time. The root was dead. Panic had been cast out. I was on the road to full recovery. When these feelings come now, they have lost their power to hurt me. When the Holy Spirit deals with such forces, he breaks their power to hurt and keep you bound.

At the end of the last century and the beginning of this one, more and more women in the world were beginning to stir. They were beginning to ask 'why?'. They began to question male dominance in almost everything from house ownership to contraception; from education to the vote. At every level they began to wake up to the awful bondage which had been inflicted upon them: the sense of being owned, the feeling of being second class, inferior and deficient. Tragically, the church which should have been pioneering, not only in emancipation but in every area of life and living, had little or no voice at all. What is worse, such voice as it did have, with a few exceptions like the Salvation Army, was bigoted, dogmatic, chauvinistic and blind. It was left to the women in the world to take the initiative. The women in the church could not. Even God, it seemed, was against them and for the 'status quo', or so they were told.

Thus, we in this century have seen the birth of the feminist movement, but surely this gives us Christians no great satisfaction. Like many other women, I have no desire to be militant, I have no ambition to be superior to men. I simply want the opportunity to be me! This particular movement in its most extreme form says that women don't need men for anything. Should you want a child, you can go to a sperm bank and be artificially inseminated and so have your baby. The father is of no account. Who wants to know who he was anyway? It is irrelevant. As far as I am concerned there is a demonic spirit at work here. This approach is as great a travesty of what God intends as severe male domination has been in the past. Jesus must be shown to be the answer to all women's difficulties. We, in the church, must get our act together and expose the problem as Enemy activity. It is not a battle for supremacy between the sexes. We can never expect to be relevant to the greater part of humanity, or to see this fortress of Satan completely rased to the ground, unless we work together.

The place of women in the church seems to be fast becoming one of the major issues of the decade. Church councils are debating it, votes are being taken and some feel it could split the Church of England from top to bottom. The people of the world listen in with unbelief as some denominations decide that women are unfitted for even certain simple tasks. They laugh at our inconsistencies. We are told that we cannot have a woman priest consecrating the bread and wine, yet the same church allows a woman prime minister to endorse the selection of its bishops and has a queen as its head. I really don't want to see the church divided for that gives yet another victory to the Enemy and however bad things get, feminism is no more of an answer today than chauvinism has been in the past. The domination of one sex over another, of one class over another, or of one colour over another, can never be God's answer. Only in coming together, never in schism, can we lovingly and truthfully look at the situation and see things through to a conclusion.

In the church we have been taught that it was the woman who was deceived and is therefore more gullible and in danger of being misled. This sin disqualifies her from certain areas of activity in the life and work of the church. Even supposing this idea were completely true, where does forgiveness and redemption come in? My Bible teaches me that my sins, although blood red, shall be as white as snow. Restoration accompanies forgiveness so that I can function fully as my Father intended. Anyway, man also sinned. In fact, in Romans chapter 5 verses 12–21 Paul puts the responsibility for sin squarely on Adam's shoulders. It could be argued that his sin was the greater, for he was not deceived but acted in the full knowledge of what he was doing. God spoke to him and instructed him personally in the Garden before the woman was formed.

With this seeming bias against women in the church, does this mean that disparity begins here at the cross? Are we saying that God's judgements are purely on the basis of sex and have nothing to do with the severity of the sin? On the contrary, the Bible does not give us this understanding. God is consistently righteous and true in all his ways. I know that we humans find it almost impossible not to grade sin. We even find comfort in the fact that the crimes of others seem worse than ours, but God sees sin for what it is. His punishments are just and he is equally forgiving when faced with a repentant heart. So where does the concept of a disqualification in the case of women come from? Has the Lord made an exception as far as deception is concerned? Is deception the one sin for which restoration can never be complete? And what of men who are deceived?

Recently, I looked into the origins of nineteen cults and false religions ranging from the Moonies to Freemasonry. It was very interesting to discover that seventeen of the nineteen were founded by men. The odd ones out were Christian Science, founded by Mary Eddy Baker over a century ago, and Spiritualism, founded in 1848 by the three Fox sisters. These two out of the nineteen are invariably the ones which are used to prove the deception argument. The other seventeen are carefully overlooked. Re-reading the story of the Fall in Genesis 3 also throws more light on the subject. I had always thought that if you were prone to being deceived you didn't know it and found it very hard to acknowledge. But when the Lord showed Eve how she had failed, she certainly knew it and fully accepted responsibility for what she had done. From Adam, however, there was no such immediate response. But more of this later.

So this attitude and teaching has been just one more bar of the cage in which so many women have found themselves. With all these problems deep in the roots of our society, our families, our genes and our church, it is fairly easy to comprehend why such a large number of us are crippled with low self-esteem. Perhaps all this may help to explain why we are never satisfied with our shape or the contours of our face; why we resent correction and discipline and why we feel that church is so often just a religious version of the captivity we have experienced in the world. But Satan is losing ground. He is being exposed for what he is. As we see his design and his vulnerability, perhaps we can turn our fears and frustration into aggression and draw upon the Holy Spirit's strength to oppose him at every turn.

This then is my background, my heritage, my chains and my scars, all of which make me and my sisters part of a damaged sex. Damaged, let me say again, not directly by flesh and blood, but by the present ruler of this world. I almost feel I should compose a chorus on this theme to be sung after each paragraph I write. I'd keep inserting, 'Sing chorus here, please!' for there is absolutely no way I want to do battle with my brothers for any hurt they may have caused. My desire is to see men and women on the same side against our common opponent; against the one who has caused us to inflict such hurt and pain upon one another. With the Holy Spirit's enabling, let's bring our family life into order, let's get our genes under control and let's see the whole church working together. For together we are a formidable army and we can establish an outpost of God's kingdom in advance of Jesus' return.

4

Men Are Also Damaged

Now let's turn our attention to the men and examine some of the areas in which the Enemy has been at work in their lives. Here we find to some extent a reflection or reversed image of the damage we have seen in women—although, of course, there are also some real differences. Before I begin though we are agreed, aren't we, that not one of us is perfect? In that case I should be able to share a few of the imperfections in the other half of God's creation, without fearing that anyone will want to stone me!

In contrast to women many men have a feeling of rightness, of being number one, of having certain inalienable rights. They may not be consciously thinking these things, but put it to a group of them and, if they are honest, a large percentage will agree to this. As a sex they grow up feeling not only physically stronger, but also superior to women in almost every way. Jewish men were traditionally encouraged to pray this prayer every day: 'I thank you, Lord, that you have not made me a Gentile, a slave or a woman.' Often men find themselves in a dilemma within their families as they usually want sons. This can become of paramount importance. Usually in spite of this they find themselves loving their daughters while bemoaning the girls' sex.

In some cultures the necessity for sons is of such concern that a man has grounds for divorce should his wife be perverse enough to produce only daughters. Recently I was in hospital and had some terrific opportunities to speak with some Muslim women. This very issue of sons came up in a rather dramatic way. One patient had become suicidal and was in a terrible emotional state. The ward sister asked me if I could help her. (By this time the staff knew about my faith and I had already had occasions to pray with some of the patients.) This particular woman had four children. In her culture, however, she only had one that counted: the boy. After two ectopic pregnancies she could have no more children and in her situation this was a disaster. She shared her fears that she would be divorced by her husband, and that her future would be black indeed. She had no other place to go and would probably end up as a slave to his new wife. How tragic that Satan can so damage such a large section of the world's male population that they see their women purely as male-child producing machines. My story has a happy ending. In this case the woman's husband told her that he had no plans to divorce her at all. Nevertheless, this kind of thing is happening in Britain today.

I know you can argue in such extreme cases about the ethnic culture and that it doesn't always apply, but if men were to share their feelings honestly, I believe we would discover that there is far more of this under the surface than we imagine. It's not something a man can sit down and explain—this feeling that sons are better. Lots of men would be ashamed and find it hard to confess to even a hint of it in their thinking. Nevertheless, for many it is a real concern. Of course, when a man begins to open up to the Holy Spirit and gets beyond his shame, God can begin the work of healing. When he faces this discovery about himself, anger may result before the desire comes to see things put right. But the desire to take back this ground from the Enemy must become the driving force, not shame. Shame makes us dumb and keeps us as we are. Shame is a powerful weapon in the Devil's armoury. We must have nothing to do with it.

It is also a fact that most men consider that the female of the species should understand that they are 'God's gift' to woman. Men don't usually feel that they will be left on the shelf. Bachelors are viewed in a totally different light to spinsters. Bachelors are thought to have chosen their state, whereas spinsters have been rejected. Whoever heard of an 'eligible spinster'? Men have the inherited right to choose a mate, and we still live in a culture which, by and large, expects the man to 'pop the question'. This can become very difficult for the poor fellow if he can't make up his mind. Is it God's will? Will it last? Is she the right girl? Does she appreciate my hobbies? By the time some men have worked it all out they are collecting their old age pension.

I had a young man in our fellowship come to share something with me. He was not coping at all with some of the girls (and I emphasise the 'some'), who were asking *him* out! Do I hear an indrawn breath or two, or a few nervous giggles? What on earth are Christian women doing asking men out? Have you ever asked yourself who set up this code of behaviour in the first place? Just because it's our cultural norm, does that make it a God-given principle of life? I don't believe so, any more than I believe that God is an Englishman and the language of heaven is the Authorised Version. The truth was that my young friend had difficulty coping with girls who he didn't find attractive asking him out.

His chest would have swollen inches and he would have been greatly flattered had the opposite been the case. My initial reply to his complaint was 'hard cheese'. I did, however, take time to explain his conditioning to him and fairly gently pointed out that women have been having to cope with this particular embarrassment for quite some time—like centuries! We have been expected to feel honoured by the condescension of the male who singles us out regardless of his acceptability or attractiveness to us.

This may seem a small thing, but even so it represents a whole way of thinking which has been dumped on us from our culture and has nothing to do with godly values. I am continuing my efforts to break the mould and encourage girls, with modesty, sometimes to be willing to take the initiative and ask a boy out for a meal, or to the cinema. After all, they both earn round about the same salary these days. In fact some girls earn more. Why should the men always be expected to foot the bill?

Another area which shows only too well how differently men and women view themselves, can be seen in our attitudes to food. When a woman reads a menu, regardless of her shape, fat or thin, she will translate her meal into calories and often choose accordingly. Most men would be hard pushed to tell you how many calories anything had. Women expect to be valued for how they measure up to the 'perfect shape', whatever that illusive thing might be.

Similar attitudes are displayed in marriage. The majority of men have an inbuilt belief that they are natural lovers, with an instinct for sex and its enjoyment. Sadly this is just not true. This inner witness within himself that he can't get it wrong, the 'Adonis syndrome' I call it, makes it difficult for him to understand why a woman dissolves into laughter at the sight of her man in his Y-fronts and socks. Not at all sexy, just very funny. Men are often puzzled when, just as they are 'raring to go' a woman will start talking about bad breath or armpit odour. Particularly young men have the idea that it is masculine not to worry about such things. They and their presence should be enough to make their wives swoon with desire. Here again we see the Enemy's work. It is called an inflated ego or more simply—pride. Marriages flounder on the rocks of these wrong attitudes as the woman's laughter turns to guilt and finally bitterness over the lack of sensitivity and romance. The man retires to nurse his bruises and sulk like a hurt child.

Another area of weakness which men suffer from is an overwhelming desire to 'pass the buck'. They often have a difficult time making decisions. It isn't that they don't know what they want to do, but they want both understanding and agreement from the women in their lives about the conclusions they reach. They want to be popular. The result can be one of two things. Either they don't make a decision at all, or they allow circumstances or someone else to make it for them. Both are equally damaging. In the first place the woman is frustrated and the man feels inwardly that he has missed the boat; in the second he feels cheated and is perpetually disappointed. Frequently, men will delay making a decision. They marshal all the facts, then they think about them. They procrastinate, expecting that other circumstances will emerge which will change or save them from facing the issue. They place the matter under consideration in the secret but forlorn hope that if they do nothing the difficulty will disappear. No such luck!

Our communities are riddled with male indecision. We find it everywhere in our society. There are endless stories of men gone fishing, golfing, footballing or to the pub, while all else—exams, homes, doorhandles which need replacing, job hunting, birth and death—is placed on the back burner in the vain expectation that everything will 'pan out'. We find it in our churches. Here the deacons are debating eternal issues, such as, should the new curtains for the meeting room be blue or red? Should the chairs have a holder for a Bible only or a Bible and hymn book? The fact that the meetings are not going anywhere and the unconverted are going to hell gets put where? On the back burner. We find it in our families. Your son wants a lift with his friends to the disco. He can't tell you when he wants it or for how many, because if he makes a decision how does he know if his mates will turn up when he suggests? If he tells them they have a lift and they are thirty minutes late, how will he cope as Dad is now eating supper with Mum and the lift is no longer forthcoming? He doesn't commit himself. It all goes—yes, you know where—on the back burner! Ignore it and it may go away, or work out all right in the end. Whatever you do don't make a decision in case it turns out to be an unpopular one.

How about the distrust that many men have for the intangible, the inexplicable, the fanciful and the intuitive things which in the main are feminine traits? All men are fully aware that life should be logical, sensible, rational and reasonable. Can't you see Thomas, the disciple, fitting perfectly into the male fraternity? There he was, he'd heard Mary's story. She had gone to the tomb where they laid Jesus, and found it empty. Well, obviously the corpse had been removed—probably by the two chaps she saw sitting on the boulder. No problem there, but then the wretched woman goes on to tell him that Jesus is alive! She'd seen one of the gardeners and when he spoke to her she believed it was the Lord. Of course, when some of the other *men* got there, he had disappeared, hadn't he? Bit of a tall story this when we all know that Jesus is dead. Proof is what Thomas needed: seeable, tangible, touchable proof. How good God is! Thomas got his proof and also a little something to think about as far as his logic was concerned. Read John 20:24–29 to check the story for yourself. When we cancel out the intuitive and the unpredictable with the logical and reasonable we have effectively silenced and dismissed fifty per cent of God's character and half of his creation.

Add to all this a fear of being dominated, not only by women but also by other men, and you begin to understand the independence which is clearly seen in the lives of so many men. They are secretive or defensive about things for fear of takeover. There is a recent TV commercial starring George Cole of Arthur Daly fame. It's all about money and savings. You know the one? In this particular scenario, Arthur is running away from his wife and hiding so 'she can't get the readies'. If you don't see how damaging this kind of portrayal is to a man's self-image you'll laugh, and we are told that when we laugh we identify. Mind you, if you don't laugh you may want to cry.

Our Enemy gets enjoyment from these problems as they are manifested in the church. Here we are often ranged on opposite sides, slogging it out, separated from one another by the history and lies with which we've been lumbered. What a sorry state we are in and how Satan loves it. Our Father wants his whole creation to come to maturity in his church. The awful situation as it exists grieves him deeply. For him to watch what should have been the crowning glory of his creative work, man, male and female, at odds with themselves, causes him endless pain. Genesis 2:23 is a recognition of oneness which should never have been destroyed by Enemy activity: 'This is now bone of my bones and flesh of my flesh; she shall be called 'woman', for she was taken out of man.' God has work for us all to do. We don't need to be concerned in case there isn't enough to go round. There's a whole world out there to be reached and we are still being bamboozled into 'in-fighting'. Thus our effectiveness is taken away and we run around in ever-decreasing circles playing at church, trying not to show how hurt, insecure and lost we are feeling.

Satan has done an excellent job of keeping men and women apart and convincing us to tighten the lid on our problems. In the church some men would view it as a serious loss of face or status and a threat to their manhood to admit to weakness. The thought of opening up or sharing with someone outside of their situation their difficulties, whether within marriage, friendship, business or fellowship, is like the prospect of walking through a brick wall or running a marathon over broken glass. 'Keep it to yourself,' comes the whisper. 'What will people think?' When a Christian marriage, business or church is floundering and outside help is suggested, the reaction can be quite violent. 'How can you be so disloyal? It's like washing our dirty linen in public. Surely we can work it out on our own!' The truth is that few of us can work it out on our own. The Enemy will not allow it and he's skilled in the art of keeping us at loggerheads. He will always try to make it impossible for us to accept help or to work it out for ourselves and so he immobilises us completely. At all costs Satan wants to keep us in conflict and ineffective-ness.

Yes, you may lose face if you admit your need; you may come crashing down from your pedestal; you may find some people are disillusioned with you, but you will also win an important battle. You will take ground away from your Opponent. You will be free and you will have begun to live as God wants, walking in the

light with one another. Read Matthew 18:15–20 to see
that God does not want issues to stand between us. He
gives us the procedures for dealing with our differences.
In Matthew 5:23 Jesus made it clear that nothing of any
kind should hinder our relationships. Men and women
of God must go on to the offensive together. Let us
reject the status quo and ditch hindering history and
tradition which does not come from the Holy Spirit or
from God-breathed Scripture. We must make as many
inroads into the Enemy's territory as we possibly can. I
want to hear the Devil screaming with rage and frustration! Working together to this end will bring security,
freedom and hope to our brothers and sisters in the
church everywhere.

5

However Did We Get into This Terrible Mess?

If we are to take our places in God's design and God's kingdom, we need to know his mind. We also need to see where and when things went wrong, and why. Then perhaps we will begin to understand some of the implications for us in our situation. I overheard my husband talking to a friend of ours, Clive Calver. He said, 'Christine doesn't have an ounce of theology in her, she just believes God.' It's true I have to rely heavily on others in this area, and here is something I have learned from my theological pals. If you want to get to the root of a truth go to the first mention of it in the Bible. The first mention can show you much about the basic foundation on which the concepts surrounding that truth are built. Well, you can't go further back than Genesis, and it was to this book I turned to learn something more about why God created men and women. From this account in the opening verses of Scripture we can see that the relationship between men and women is, itself, foundational in God's scheme of things. To ignore or fail to understand this will seriously hinder our appreciation of the rest of the Bible.

By the way, how do you read your Bible? I've dis-

covered that even the way in which you approach the
Bible can be unique to you. I was taught that you read
the Bible and then you are to think about what you've
read. If you did this properly, light would break and
understanding would come. This, of course, works
excellently for many people. It just didn't work for me.
I would read the words, then I'd try to think about
them. I soon discovered that I thought very little, sometimes nothing at all. Generally speaking, for me, words
conjure up pictures and somehow when reading the
Bible I had come to believe that this was unacceptable.
Once I realised that this lie was robbing me of something which had been special to me, I decided to be
myself and let the pictures come. I soon regained the
joy and thrill of reading God's word again and I also
found that I was actually understanding it as well.

When I read the story of creation over again I asked
myself, 'What do I see?' rather than, 'What does it say?'
Wonderful pictures began to form in my mind. When
you come across the tremendous descriptions of God in
Scripture do you try to picture him? For me, at times,
this unbearable light pours into my mind; at other
times thunder and fire roll over me. In the creation
story God seems to me to be a heavy, coloured liquid,
bright with light, able to separate himself from himself.
So I have a picture of this liquid God. It all sounds
rather peculiar when it's written down, but I realised
that it tied in with other scriptures I'd read concerning
God being light, and his wisdom being multi- or rain-
bow-coloured. I became quite excited about what I was
seeing. This God who was talking to himself and send-
ing a part of himself out to brood over the waters in
Genesis 1:2 decides to make a being just like himself.
Genesis 1:26–28 says, 'Let us make man in our image,
in our likeness, and let *them* rule.' These were the
Maker's instructions on the packet and they're still

there, written on our hearts today. So we have been made in God's image, with his likeness, designed by him to rule and reign.

Hang on a minute, it's getting a bit confusing here. God seems to make this creation as fluid as he is. One moment he's speaking in the singular, the next in the plural. One minute it's man and now it's male and female. What is going on here, are we really like this God? Oh, I know all about Genesis 2 being a detailed look at the sixth day, and that all the obscurities can be wonderfully explained if you understand the deeper meaning of the Hebrew. Sometimes I wonder if, in our clinical approach, we explain away the mystery. After all, the Bible wasn't just written for intellectuals, it was also penned for ordinary folk like me and you. Could it be that in a single act of creation God put together what we would think of as a composite being having all the godly characteristics, both masculine and feminine? The mind boggles and being the person I am, the pictures forming in my mind almost defy description. It does begin to make sense though, because when God saw that his 'one-off' man was lonely, he had quite a puzzle to solve.

The Lord had made man in his own image. He couldn't doodle in the dirt again or hunt around for some left-overs from the other days of creation. He had used everything up, the sugar and spice and all things nice, *and* the slugs and snails and puppy dogs tails! His work was finished. By the seventh day, the Bible says, God had completed his work and rested. In other words the job was totally finished, perfectly completed. It wasn't a leap year with a day left over in which to make something else. So what did God do? After looking at all the animals and finding no suitable mate, he took his composite human, he put them to sleep and he divided them up. From the one being, God made male and female in his image. So Eve was not an afterthought, a kind of 'spare rib' Chinese take away, she was a whole side of man's nature. No longer was either man or woman fully representative of all God's attributes. Alone each is incomplete but together, and only together, can they become the true reflection of the character of God. They were designed by him and made in his likeness to rule and reign over all the creation. In all of history Jesus was the only exception as Paul records in Colossians 2:9—'In Christ all the fulness of the Deity lives in bodily form.'

I like to picture the original man in the garden and to imagine his loneliness without a companion. Adam named all the animals and watched them at play, seeing that each had a counterpart, but none could relate to him as an equal. Adam enjoyed planting the daffodils and tulips to make a colourful display. Adam knew when to sow lettuce seeds, tomatoes and onions, and when to harvest them all. He knew how to bake, freeze and bottle everything. There was nothing he couldn't do. He was complete but alone. Adam's arrangements of colour and texture in the garden were beautiful. The flower arrangements were a joy to behold. He listened with bated breath to the bird songs, played with the animals, drank from the same sparkling waters as the lion. When God came into the garden calling, 'Adam,' he went running to walk, talk and enjoy his Master's company in that glorious paradise. Adam, like God, was complete.

When the Lord God was not in the garden Adam had no one with whom to communicate, no one to share his thoughts. He could not cry out like you or me, 'Look at that sunset,' or, 'See those young puppies at play together.' Adam talked only to Adam when God was not around. He had no one to laugh with, no one to play with, no one with whom he could make love. God saw this and said, 'It is not good for the man to be alone' (Gen 2:18). So he put Adam to sleep, divided him up and gave him a friend. Isn't that what God is looking for in us, friends to share with? From here on, when God came and walked in the garden calling, 'Adam,' two people ran to meet him. At that time Eve didn't even have a separate name, she was only called Eve after the Fall. It's a wonderful picture, isn't it? One name and all mankind responding to God. It's tremendous to be unique as individuals, but we also need to discover our corporate identity again. Surely we see this story re-enacted in its ultimate form in Jesus' sleep of death on the cross. From the wound opened up in his side, a bride was formed to enjoy eternity with him. As joint heirs with Christ we are called to be rulers together, not only over the earthly realm, but in heaven as well.

God's heart towards Jesus his Son is to provide a helpmeet suitable for this task. The church today is being prepared to fulfil that role alongside Jesus, just as Eve was God's provision for Adam. In Genesis 2:18–20 the Lord God said, 'It is not good for the man to be alone. I will make a helper suitable for him.' Later it also says, 'But for Adam no suitable helper was found.'

When we look elsewhere for this same word, 'help-meet' or 'helper', we find Moses using it in Exodus 18:4. Here the text says, 'My father's God was my *helper*; he saved me from the sword of Pharaoh.' Often, I have heard the argument that this word 'helpmeet', when used in connection with Eve, denotes woman's inferiority or subjection to man. How can this be true when the same word used in other scriptures is used of God in an identical way? Deuteronomy 33:29, speaking of God says, 'Blessed are you, O Israel! Who is like you, a people saved by the Lord? He is your shield and *helper* and your glorious sword.' The Psalms are full of references to God as our helper or helpmeet. The same Hebrew root word is used in all these examples. Could we ever, in any circumstances, see God as being inferior or subject to anyone or anything? Maybe some of us need to take another look at our definition here and allow ourselves a little adjustment in our thinking. God's original intention was for the woman to be a helper in full fellowship and harmony with the man.

Now enters the villain of the piece. Talk about divided we fall! Genesis really does underline the need for the unity of God's creation. No wonder Jesus was preoccupied with this in his prayer in John chapter 17! Well, I'm sure you know the story. After listening to the serpent's lies, the woman takes the fruit and eats. She then gives it to the man who also eats, thus they both sin. It's really interesting that even at this moment in the account, the togetherness of the pair comes across. Genesis 3:6–7 says, 'She also gave some to her husband, who was with her, and he ate it. Then the eyes of both of them were opened.' It was only after they had both eaten that they understood what they had done and that they were naked. Such was their unity.

Following their disobedience they heard the Lord God walking in the garden and hid themselves from him. When he called their name this time, they were afraid. Their sin was out in the open, and God demands an explanation. He calls to the man, 'Have you eaten from the tree that I commanded you not to eat from?' The man immediately replies, 'The woman you put here with me—she gave me some fruit from the tree, and I ate it' (Gen 3:11–12). Here is the very first time in history that a man passed the buck, and Adam did so in two ways. First, he blamed the woman and secondly, God. It was a two-way side-step. With one hand he pointed to the woman and with the other to God. 'Don't blame me, Lord,' is what he is saying. 'The woman you gave me is responsible. Sort it out between the two of you.' Then the Lord God turned to the woman enquiring, 'What is this you have done?' The woman shamefully but readily admits, 'The serpent deceived me and I ate' (Gen 3:13–14). She is absolutely clear in her reply and accepts the responsibility, 'I ate.'

It must have been quite a scene. Adam blaming everyone but himself, the woman filled with the knowledge of her sin and the serpent rubbing his hands with glee. Not only had the Enemy succeeded in separating God from his creation, but he had separated the two sides of the creation, one from the other. What a victory. What a triumph for him and what a thing to celebrate!

Hold on, though, it's not over yet. God is speaking again in Genesis 3:14–19. Now he is laying down some pretty serious consequences. The serpent is cursed and condemned to crawl on his belly. To this day the woman and her descendants hate his kind. She will have trouble in child-bearing and her husband will rule over her. This is the first mention of a husband ruling over his wife and came as part of God's judgement on the woman. It was never in God's original plan that this should happen. It was part of the outcome and result of sin. The earth itself is also cursed because of the man. He will have to work hard to provide food by the sweat of his brow until he dies. One promise, and only one, is given in the midst of all this cursing and it is to the woman. Her offspring will finally triumph and mortally wound the serpent. When he was done, God banished them from the garden. 'Cruel,' you say? Not at all. In so doing God preserved them from eating of the tree of life and so living for ever in their sinful state. They would then have been as the fallen angels for whom there is no redemption.

Now I'd like to identify a few of the threads from this story and trace them forward in time. Let's look first at the serpent or lizard as he was. Today, snakes travel on their bellies, they can climb trees but never have been able to balance on their tails. In this creeping state they positively eat dirt and remain a symbol of evil to all mankind. Another interesting thought is that women, in particular, dislike snakes, and with some the fear even includes worms. Satan obviously took on this form in the garden and as an intelligent being was able to speak and reason. This event has left a scar deep in the very soul of women. Imagine the panic when Satan hears God's promise of a Son to the woman. A Son who would one day depose and eradicate him. He looked at the woman with tremendous hatred and began to put his evil plan into action. He, the serpent, would take up God's curse and work with it using it in every way he possibly could. He would seek to persecute the woman and destroy her seed.

God put no time scale on the birth of the Child who was to destroy Satan. His arrival could have been immediate, or at least within nine months. The Enemy looked at Eve with fresh eyes. Only she could bring about his ultimate downfall, and savagely he attacked her very femininity. He went for her womb, her menstrual cycle and her womanhood, especially the reproductive organs. Any pregnant woman was his special target. How could he tell which woman would produce his executioner and the Son who would bring his reign to an end? If we follow the Devil's attacks on women through history, we shall see his consistent working on the reproductive functions, the emotions and the act of child-bearing. Women became prisoners of their own bodies in the very world that was created for them. Men have been manipulated to join in the abuse and have come to view women as unreliable because of their emotional reactions. We are unpredictable and untrustworthy. At certain times in the month we may not be considered to be in our right minds.

This is a very black picture, although not all women are affected so deeply. Nevertheless, many do admit to the truth of what I'm saying in some measure or other. In both the Old and New Testaments we see examples of Satan's panic and the resulting barbarism, as again and again he murdered women and their babies in an effort to destroy the Seed. Is it any wonder that centuries of continuous warfare should have produced the fears and phobias as we see in women? The wonder is that things are not a dozen times worse.

Who was behind Pharaoh's decree in Exodus 1:16–22 that all male babies were to be killed at birth? Pharaoh may have given his reason for doing so as population control, but we know differently. Satan was afraid the Deliverer would come, and in one sense he did. Moses survived to lead the Children of Israel out of Egypt.

We have heard this same argument many times in history. Again and again we see Satan, in his fear, striking out at mothers and their babies. In Matthew 2:13–18 we read how Joseph was warned to flee into Egypt with Jesus and Mary. The reason was to preserve the baby's life as Herod had ordered the death of all male babies in Bethlehem. Was it really just Herod who was running scared after hearing about the angels singing to the shepherds and the reasons for the journey of the Magi?

There is an evil principle at work here. Satan's enemy is still a woman pregnant with a male child. Today, we face the same threat. True, Jesus has been born to Mary and, yes, he has completed his task. Jesus is ruling and reigning in the heavenlies—but! The church of Jesus Christ, his virgin bride here on earth, is now the woman to whom Satan directs his hatred. Just as the Holy Spirit came upon Mary, so he is coming upon the church today and she is heavy with a male child. Every fresh movement of the Holy Spirit in the church is, in essence, just like Jesus being born into the world through his people. Satan is under threat and is once more anxious to destroy this child. Revelation 12 confirms the truth of this when it speaks of a woman, clothed with the sun, who gives birth to a man child. Standing by is the dragon ready to devour the child as soon as it is born. The child, who is destined to rule the nations, is caught up to God and to his throne. From there he makes war against the dragon and his angels and prevails through 'the blood of the lamb and by the word of their testimony; they did not love their lives'. What a picture for us as Christ's church called to bring about the serpent's final defeat. No wonder Satan hates pregnant women.

In the light of these facts, Christian women must learn to confront their Enemy. We must deny him the right to expect passive co-operation from us. We should begin to pray for freedom from menstrual tensions. We should demand the right to enjoy our babies and delight in the prospect of the Devil's ultimate downfall from the fruit of the womb of the church. Let us expect to be in control of our minds and emotions for 365 days each year, and by God's grace we will learn, in peace and humility, to rule and reign with Jesus through service and sacrifice.

I promised that I would take a closer look at the menstrual cycle in the light of Satan's plan. I have already said that our Enemy, in his fear and anger, attacked women particularly in their sexuality and reproductive system. His desire was to use this as a foundation to the wall of separation between men and women. Increasingly in the media, the problems of pre-

and post-menstrual tension, and ovulation tension, are being discussed and analysed. We hear harrowing tales of complete personality changes during these 'times of the month'. At the very worst end of the spectrum, a woman can be considered to be emotionally unstable and out of her mind. At best she can suffer mild discomfort and irritability. For many this has been a real cause for concern, and has led to a distrust of women in places of responsibility. To be honest, is it any wonder that at these times women cannot be trusted, when they are likely to hit out irrationally, hurting those around them. When the storm has once again passed over, they can be left either puzzled and condemned by their own behaviour and reactions, or shrugging their shoulders until the next time. Both can lead to more pain and misunderstanding. So what is the answer?

Several solutions are offered to their problems. Medication has brought relief to countless women but, in some cases, it does have an adverse side effect of dependency. Others have found the problem alleviated by the careful use of vitamin tablets. Some symptoms can be caused by vitamin deficiency, which is not unthinkable in this day and age, with so much processed and fast food being consumed.

However, for me, the answer came when I began to recognise the Enemy's handiwork. I could fully accept the rise and fall of certain hormones in my body. I understood the process which caused me to menstruate in a regular cycle. The thing I could not receive was the inevitability of the distress and turmoil, which left me and my loved ones in such pain. The day I saw where this came from was the day I kicked Satan out. In other words I refused to believe that this syndrome was a part of the 'woman's lot'. I don't want to over-simplify what happened, and I acknowledge that healing is a process that often takes time. There can be much to pray

through, perhaps with friends. And we must acknowledge that, even after this kind of prayer warfare, some
women do not see complete healing in this area. At the
end of the day, God is sovereign in this as in all matters.

But don't let that discourage you. There are others
who, like me, have found healing. Strangely, some of
you will experience feelings of panic at the prospect of
being released. Take courage. That too is a response to
the years of conditioning. To baulk and turn away is
understandable if not right. Once free from the emotional switchback, there are responsibilities to be faced.
You will find that some of your reactions are ungodly
and need to be disciplined. Gone are the days when an
explosion or a torrent of tears can be simply brushed
aside or excused with, 'It's the time of the month!' Now
these outbursts must be treated as sin, and sin needs
repentance. We women must go to war on the residue of
satanic programming with the whole of our hearts.
Then we will begin to cope with the cut and thrust of
discussion and dialogue in the company of men, without the disgrace and embarrassment of constantly being
a weeping willow. We must not shy away from the
responsibility which freedom brings. Our men, who
have undergone their own conditioning from the Devil
and have coped for years with mothers, sisters and
wives who are unpredictable and volatile, may find it
difficult to believe that it is possible for us to change.
This is one of the main reasons why women are so
frequently kept out of leadership. We women are called
upon to stand in our new-found freedom, and not to
react all over the place. Who wants all that emotion
around when decisions are being made?

As usual, I may have painted a black-and-white
picture, but I feel if we are honest, most of us will
identify to some degree. Do you want this kind of
responsibility, ladies? Do you want to be answerable for

yourself and your contributions? if so, pick up the sword of God's truth and do battle on your own behalf. Cut out the cancer that threatens to destroy your spiritual growth and stems the flow of God's gifts through you. Be made whole!

At the onset of the menopause, I had to reaffirm my stand all over again. After some years of victory I began to take success for granted, and it came as a surprise when I began to experience a whole host of new symptoms, which made no sense to me at all. A range of feelings attacked me, from crying at a seagull on the TV screen, to my face going numb or my whole body breaking out in a sweat at the most inconvenient moment. My first course of action was to dump all these symptoms on the doctor. I have great cause to be thankful to the medical profession and praise God for their gifts and abilities, but one thing I have come to understand is that they are not actually God! Doctors are mortals just like everyone else. With experience I have learned to mistrust one particular phrase: 'It's only natural.' When I hear that, I know to be on my guard.

So here I am in the surgery, having shared with the doctor my chapter of woes. His answer: 'Well, it's only natural!'

'Oh, is it?' thinks I.

'You see,' he continues, 'most of these are recognised symptoms of the menopause.'

Now I don't want to cause any of you unnecessary pain, but I do want to share my experience honestly, for if God can do it for one, it proves he can do it for others. Enlisting the help of John, over the next few months, we prayed together, particularly when I was experiencing acute distress, and slowly but surely reclaimed the ground. With the passage of time I ended up in hospital where I had the whole of my reproductive system removed. After the operation, the surgeon told me what

I should expect and how to cope with these new symptoms. He reassured me by saying, 'This is quite natural. Your body has had a shock and an instant conclusion to your menopause.' You can imagine my reaction to that statement. Well, God is really good, and now more than two years after the event I have experienced none of those symptoms at all.

Thank the Lord that the Holy Spirit is alive today, revealing God to us. There is no way we can pull ourselves up by our own bootlaces. However, when the Spirit illuminates some way in which he wants to work, he also gives us the ability and faith to co-operate. Jesus is always the answer to our difficulties. When we find him, even if the problem does not go away, somehow it loses its sting in the face of his endless, botomless, fathomless, ever-present love.

Another obvious outcome of God's curse can be seen on the land. This is self-evident. Any patch of ground left to itself for a season will grow a fine crop of weeds. Anyone labouring in agriculture fights a constant battle with insects, pest and blight as well as thorns and thistles, and that's apart from the quality of the ground. Modern insecticides and fertilisers are not always all they promise to be. Sometimes they end up doing more harm than good in disturbing the balance of nature and poisoning our bodies.

The rigid divisions in the family, between who works and who stays at home, are becoming more and more blurred in our particular culture. Until this last eighty years it has always been clear: men went out to work and women stayed at home. For centuries man has been the breadwinner and has supported the young, the old and the females in his household. It is true that everyone had their sphere of activity, but the main burden of responsibility rested upon the male. This burden brought either riches and power when the land yielded favourably, or poverty and despair in famine. In both situations men were distanced from their women through pride or guilt. They seldom really shared their joys and sorrows.

So enmity came, not just between the serpent and the woman, but also between the woman and the man. That enmity has infiltrated the church of Jesus Christ. We have been subtly taught to believe that man plus God equals completeness, woman plus God equals deception. Neither is true. Man plus woman plus God is where completeness really begins. Jesus is returning for a bride, his church. This bride will be made up of all those who purify themselves and put on their beautiful garments of righteousness and praise, a mighty army of both men and women.

'Ah,' I hear some of you gentlemen and ladies saying, 'it was God who did the cursing and what he did was final. No one can change what he decrees. How do you explain that?' Well, that is certainly true, but God did not intend the curse to remain. His desire has always been to remove the curse and to reinstate us to the place he created us to occupy and even take us beyond that place. His discipline was a means to an end, not an end in itself. We see this reflected in the law in the Old Testament. Women were unclean while menstruating, which meant that most women were in a defiled state for a major part of their lives. They were also unclean after childbirth, longer for a girl than for a boy. That was the law and the law came as a result of the Fall. Yes, our whole gender was cursed and in bondage. This was the outcome of our sin, but meanwhile God was instituting his long-term plan. He prepared and sent his Son Jesus to take upon himself my curses and yours. In him those curses are themselves cursed and no longer apply. Galatians 3:13 says, 'Christ redeemed us from the curse of the law by becoming a curse for us.' Jesus died and carried these curses into hell and he left them there when he rose again, so obliterating the divisions in his church.

In Christ there are now no divisions of race, class or sex. 'There is neither Jew nor Greek, slave nor free, male nor female, for you are all one in Christ Jesus' (Gal 3:28). If these divisions continue to exist in the church, then Jesus hasn't gained the response he desires, and until he does he'll not return. In John 17:20–21 Jesus prayed, 'My prayer is not for them alone,' referring to his disciples. 'I pray also for those who will believe in me through their message, that all of them may be one, Father, just as you are in me and I am in you. May they also be in us so that the world may believe that you have sent me.' This is the one prayer above all others uttered in history that is going to be fulfilled and I want to be a part of it.

I trust by now you understand that I don't wish to promote a new Christian feminist movement. That is not what I'm after at all. Nothing but the best for this particular woman. I want us all to take our place and play the part that God has equipped us for in the church. For it is in the church where we shall see the true glory of Christ and all that he has accomplished, not in fragmented groups of individuals banging their own little drums. I want to pay a small tribute to my husband here as he has kept me on target in this connection and saved me from going off in all kinds of directions. Without him I don't know where I would be. He's helped me, shouted at me, gone silent on me, taught me, shared his vision with me and suffered my constant questioning 'Why?' for thirty years. I certainly would not be as far on or as fulfilled as I am today without him. If you want to blame anyone for this book, I'll supply his name and address.

From all that took place in the Genesis story two

patterns of behaviour were set in motion. On Eve's admission of guilt, Adam's reaction was, 'It was the woman's fault. She lost paradise and she's not to be trusted.' Division was justified in his mind and a path away from the woman was opened up before him. On the other hand Eve, on hearing that she was to blame, because self-centred. She believed that she was more guilty than her partner and the die was cast. There was no way back from the separation which drove her away from man—the man she should have loved.

Throughout the intervening generations from then until now, Satan has successfully driven the wedge deeper and deeper into the relationship between the sexes. At this very moment in time it seems that the gap is as wide as ever with division and divorce in marriage at its highest level. Apart from a few brief and geographically isolated periods during great revival movements of history, the futile situation has persisted. Sadly, the Enemy regained his stranglehold in these places and slowly but surely we lost the ground which had been gained. The church, which should have been the vehicle of emancipation, leading the way at all levels, has been a party to the bondage, at times even increasing and perpetuating it.

Women have also played their part in maintaining the status quo. They have withdrawn themselves and their gifts from the fray, allowing their cause to get buried under the garbage showered upon them by the Devil. When their gifts could have helped to turn the tide and alert the whole church to the danger, women refused or were unable to speak. They were muzzled by the fear of rejection, of getting it wrong or being unable to explain their feelings properly. In this connection I've been thinking through some of our own recent history in the 'house churches' of which I am a part. I've seen the pain and heartache which has been experienced as we've watched people we counted as our close friends and co-workers drawn into, what seems to me to be, blind alleys and cul-de-sacs. I've asked myself and the Lord, what it is that keeps the women in these situations, some of whom I know to be sensitive and intuitive people, from calling out to their men, 'Stop! Hold on a minute! Aren't we rushing into a siding?' Or at least, 'Are we here by design, to regroup and move out again?' Perhaps they have asked these questions and received satisfactory answers, or maybe they feel they can do no more about the situation. Or could it be that their historic past has so conditioned them, that they feel unable to say anything at all?

Throughout the generations of Judaism and also Christianity it has been thrust down our throats that, because of our sin and our susceptibility to deception, we women should be silent. We have been guilty of co-operating with the Enemy. We have kept quiet when sometimes we could have made all the difference. Speak to a woman about the things which have gone wrong in the family or the church. Very often she will admit to knowing where the problem lay right from the start, but because she didn't feel needed or trusted she held her tongue. Years of conditioning lie behind these reactions.

Lord, please set your people free. Free your daughters from their chains. Liberate them from their feelings of being unable to hear your voice or to speak and act for you. Take away the distorting spectacles men wear, which affect their sight and lead them astray. For Jesus' sake put an end to the garden controversy once and for all and make your people one.

6

Do Gifts and Ministries Have a Gender?

Do I smell gunpowder in the air? Do I hear daggers and swords being sharpened and guns being loaded? Perhaps I'm wrong and you are merely clearing your throats and settling yourselves more comfortably in your armchairs. If so, I'd like to look at the question as to whether gifts and ministries have a gender. How does God view women in this connection? Well, to start with I know that he likes us just about as much as he likes men. I also know that when you try to back up the worldly discrepancies in the treatment of men and women with the Scriptures, it just doesn't come off. God does not seem to have a preference for one part of his creation above another. It is quite clear to me that whether it is David or Ruth, Solomon or Deborah, John or Mary, what our Father is looking for is children whose attitude is, 'Lord, use me.' When he finds this response to him in a humble heart, regardless of sex, he goes right ahead and uses that person, even though they may be far from perfect.

Our sex, and of course by this I mean gender, obviously does come into consideration for a particular job in hand. The Lord could not have sent a man in

Esther's place, nor could he have provided a wife for Boaz without Ruth. To think otherwise would be clearly foolish. God always chooses people who are fitted for the task he wants done. I doubt very much if a woman would have got to first base in Pharaoh's court. If she had been very beautiful she might have been forced into his bed, but probably not received into his council chamber. God, however, had the ideal person prepared for the job: Moses. The servant woman Hagar gave Abraham a longed-for son, but he was illegitimate. God had already chosen the woman who was going to bear the promised child for Abraham and he kept his word, even though Sarah had the baby in her old age.

Nothing is to be second best with God. He is well able to keep his promises in every respect and always looks for the right person for the job. Even though at times he has to wait for years, he doesn't change his mind. Remember Joshua and Caleb were chosen to go into the promised land? Their efforts were thwarted the first time round, but God had his way in the end (see Num 13:1—14:38). I wonder if there was anyone else in the whole of Israel who could have done what Jael did in mustering her female aggression to overcome Sisera (Judg 4:17—22)? What a victory! But I'll come back to Jael. How about Deborah who also features in the same story (Judg 4:1—16)? I have heard a sermon or two as to how God would have preferred to use a man at this time to lead the army of Israel, but that, to me, is rubbish! God doesn't use second best. He waits for the appropriate time to bring about his purposes and he used Deborah because he had equipped her for the task.

God is the Giver of life, the great Designer and Creator. He puts us together, forms us in our mother's womb and Psalm 139 describes this fantastically. He lovingly chose the colour of our eyes. He decided whether we should be able to sing or dance, paint or act, cook an incredible meal or run a fast mile. Our God has a plan for each one of us which he worked on even before we were conceived and he has gifted us accordingly. I cannot believe that mere chance was responsible for putting any of us together. The thumb print of our Maker seen in the uniqueness of each one denies that possibility. Romans 11:29 makes it crystal clear that our gifts are from God and are given without repentance on his part. Just to be sure, I hope you understand that this means God does not snatch back the gifts he thoughtfully planted in us. For example, we have to admit that Chopin's gift was formidable, though we may not particularly like his style of music. He may never have acknowledged Christ, but at no time did God even once dream of withdrawing that amazing gift of musical genius.

What I'm seeking to underline here, is that God has taken the responsibility to fashion us to his design. Father has the whole spectrum of natural gifts before him and they come in various-sized packages. Here, for example, is singing. Singing is offered in three sizes: small, medium and large, and each size comes in low, middle or high range. Unless you are a mute, and that wouldn't be the way God made you, then every creature has at least a small gift which, however tuneless it may be, pleases our heavenly Father. Into some, though, God puts a medium or large gift. Medium means you can stay in tune and maybe harmonise a little, pleasant to the ear; but large is positively for listening to. You stay in tune, you harmonise and when the Spirit touches your vocal chords people could be forgiven for thinking it's an angel singing. You of your own volition can do nothing to get the large parcel. That's God's gift to you. What you can do is develop and improve the talent to the best of your ability, and I believe that pleases God. You have shown that you value what he has given.

The abilities you were born with are precisely the package God designed for you. Shakespeare makes the observation in *Twelfth Night* that 'some are born great, some achieve greatness and some have greatness thrust upon them'. But I say, happy are the men or women who achieve their full potential in God. Unhappy and misplaced are those who are born into or have situations thrust upon them, situations for which they are ill-prepared. They are square pegs in round holes. They live out their lives like someone who has shoes which are either cripplingly tight or foolishly large. God gives us gifts as our Father. We don't have the right to query them in ourselves or in another. We are to recognise and encourage them. In doubting them we are questioning God's wisdom. We just need to provide these God-given talents with the right soil and nutrients to grow, blossom and glorify the Lord.

Now, gifts and abilities, give or take one or two obvious exceptions, are neither male nor female and we must break down the cultural prejudices which deny this and are still firmly in place in many of our minds. The man who walks into the hospital ward and calls himself a nurse, still meets with a hesitation from many patients. A woman engineer has to run the gauntlet of incredulity and mockery as well as the genuine amazement and questions of her male counterparts. Neither nurse nor engineer are wanting to change their sex. They simply need the room to express and develop their gifts within the framework of their own lives. Here is the key to that scripture which is so often misused in connection with our youngsters, 'Train a child in the way he should go, and when he is old he will not turn from it' (Prov 22:6). Many Christians believe this refers to training a child in the faith when, in fact, it relates to encouraging his bent or gifting in life. How important it is for us not to work out our frustrated ambitions through our children, but to allow them to find their own calling and place in life.

Some folk may consider this line of argument to be dangerous. They feel that we should not encourage what seem to be masculine traits in women or feminine traits in men. Personally, I question whether we should make these kinds of definitive statements about what are male or female attributes at all. Do we really understand how much of our thinking comes down to historic and cultural conditioning? When we box people in to our ideas of what they are or are not allowed to do, we may find ourselves questioning God's creative order. We might also be opening the door to condemnation and confusion for many sincere people who just don't fit the pigeon holes we've made for them. We are so good at putting things into our little boxes and clearly labelling them 'right' or 'wrong', but by whose standards? Certainly not God's. In Britain, for example, you'll find only a handful of women farmers. We all know that farmers are men, aren't they? Statistics, however, say something very different outside of Britain. Did you realise that worldwide seventy per cent of farmers, that is those who grow food, are women? Naturally we have got it right and everyone else is out of step. How foolish we are to think this way, but many people in our country do believe that there is something essentially right and even Christian about our own way of life both in and out of the church.

We constantly try to tie God down, but he won't have it. Just when we begin to feel we've got him sorted out he does something truly amazing which defies description. The Lord has such a wonderful sense of humour. Take the intellect, for example. We all know that in the main men are logical and women intuitive.

Even I understand that. It's one of the reasons, we are told, why women don't make good leaders, although I'm not quite sure what intellect and logic necessarily have to do with godly leadership. Paul didn't always seem to rate them very highly! Anyway, John and I were watching TV over Christmas and were amused and delighted to discover that, according to David Frost and the *Guinness Book of Records*, the person with the highest IQ in the world is a woman! When will we stop telling God what he can and cannot do, particularly when it comes to the natural gifts he distributes to men and women? We really must let God be God in this, as well as every other area of life.

Father sees us as his children and he wants to shower these natural talents generously upon us. We are the ones who are always trying to tidy things up all the time. The Holy Spirit also loves us and is in the business of giving us gifts of the supernatural order. Here again I don't believe that the Spirit discriminates between male and female, black and white, rich or poor. In fact the Bible emphatically tells us that the Spirit will be poured out upon all flesh and that our sons and our daughters will prophesy (Acts 2:17; Joel 2:28). For lots of us this concept is mind-bending. We wouldn't do it that way. We'd be much more comfortable passing on rewards for good behaviour and gifts for those we deem to have deserved them. Thank God that he isn't like us. Why do we always want to cut him down to our size? God is ready, willing and able to pour out his Spirit liberally and that's great news for me and for you! It's in his nature to be miraculously generous. Jesus didn't send one of his disciples for half a dozen bottles of cheap supermarket wine to rescue the wedding. No, only 150 gallons of the very best would satisfy him. Not for him a few hundred stars, strategically placed here and there, for the inhabitants of earth to enjoy. No, myriads were flung by his free hand into every corner of space—some never to be seen by any human eye.

The Holy Spirit is going to need all our daughters, as well as our sons, if he is going to work through all flesh to bring forth a church which is worthy of Jesus. Now there's no way that I would say that God cannot use men in the realm of spiritual gifts. It would be foolish to suggest such a thing, but the fact is, there's not a great deal going on in this area, in spite of all the male activity in the church, particularly on the platform and in the leadership. Could it be that the male disposition, with its plausibility and reason, is less open to the inexplicable? My own feeling is that even if this is not true, still much of the dynamic power of the Spirit is locked up in the ladies of our churches and fellowships. They do not feel free or released or encouraged enough by the men to launch out and experiment under the watchful eye of those who oversee. There is a Christian idealism that says we have got to get it right every time and this leaves no room for error in the use of spiritual gifts. This is desperately restrictive and unrealistic.

Certainly I would not want the gifts to be used without scrutiny or proper criticism and discipline. For me that almost goes without saying. Many men who operate the gifts, and who would be cautious of women functioning in them, seem to live in a world of make believe anyway. How often do they refer back and check out that prophetic word or see whether the folk they pronounced well were really healed or not?

A woman's abilities, touched and motivated by the Holy Spirit, are indeed a fertile ground for the flow of supernatural gifts. Her intuition and openness to the unpredictable can be wonderfully anointed by God to receive words of wisdom and knowledge as well as faith, prophecy or gifts of healing. She must not, however, allow her sensitivity to be a breeding ground for fear, should her work be questioned or reviewed. We must all take responsibility for our gifts and be willing to have them examined. The Scriptures clearly teach that. But they also teach that the supernatural gifts are given, not just to men, but to each one as the Spirit sees fit (1 Cor 12:11). Philip the evangelist had four daughters spoken of in Acts 21:9, and every one of them prophesied. All a credit to the Holy Spirit and their father's ability to encourage and release them in such a male-dominated society.

In Mark 16:17, after having called his followers to world mission, Jesus then assured them that signs would follow the ministry of 'those who believe'. Faith and miracles for evangelism were not to be restricted to a favoured few, but were available to everyone who believed. Any one of his followers who believed would have the power and authority to speak in tongues, pick up serpents, overcome physical attacks on their lives and heal the sick. There is a stream of women who have gone out and claimed these promises in recent history, from Gladys Aylward to Jackie Pullinger, with thousands upon thousands of unknowns in between, in every continent of the world. May this stream continue and become a mighty river.

So we have seen that the Father has created natural gifts within us and the Spirit has poured out his supernatural abilities upon us. Now let's look at the gifts that Jesus, the Son, imparts to his church. Jesus loved us so much that he was prepared to die for us all, women included. He is also the risen Lord who gives gifts to his church. Ephesians 4:11–13 reveals these gifts as apostles, prophets, evangelists, pastors and teachers. All these ministries are needed to bring the body of Christ to maturity. We may all say 'amen' to this concept, but immediately get into difficulties when we attempt to apply it to women as well as men. Of course, we agree that women are a part of the church. In fact numerically they are usually the larger part, which may say something about their readiness to respond. However, when we talk about the five-fold ministries being open to women, we are moving into dangerous water for some.

If you believe that no woman under any circumstances should be allowed to teach men, then the gifts of the risen Christ are only available to one sex. When put like that, it may not seem fair and it may appear to be hard, but it is the logical conclusion. Nonetheless in practice we are not terribly logical at all, just reactionary I believe. In reality over the centuries in many of the revival movements women have functioned in these gifts, usually without being recognised or acknowledged. What about the army of female missionary apostles sent all round the globe even in the last two hundred years? What we are actually saying by adopting this head-in-the-sand attitude is that it's fine for a woman to function as an apostle as long as it's to foreigners. This is a hangover from our imperialist past when we felt superior as a nation. Women teachers were good enough for the colonies, other women and children, but Englishmen must keep themselves pure. Surely if women are so dangerous as teachers we should hardly let them loose on our most vulnerable members!

This attitude is reflected in the position in which a fine lady missionary I know of has found herself, as she operates in one of the most dangerous areas in the world. The mission board, made up of men, was keen to be in control of the decision-making process, but backed off when it came to visiting the field. In effect, they were saying, 'We'll do the important work of juggling the finance and the administration, while you face physical dangers of hunger, rape and death.' In my understanding, she's one of today's many women apostles. She has been prepared and sent by the Lord to help in the work of saving precious souls and building a church every bit as precious to God as our British one.

We all have to face a great danger when we are anxious to prove things, even from the Bible. It is possible, if we have the will and the determination, to find texts and isolated verses that will support almost any idea. My own concern is that we should try to look at the Bible picture as a whole, asking ourselves at the same time, 'What is God's heart in this matter of women in ministry?' Do we believe that God is seeking ways to restore us fully to himself? Or are we convinced that once God has cursed, he refuses to provide an avenue of escape? Of course we can't believe that, otherwise there would be no hope of salvation. I suppose most of us would agree that slavery is wrong, wouldn't we? I'm pretty sure there would be almost universal agreement here. But did you know, that in nineteenth-century Britain, when Wilberforce was seeking to abolish slavery, the greatest opposition came from Christians who felt absolutely clear that they could back their practice from Scripture? Not the cruelty perhaps, but certainly the practice. They believed they could justify slavery from Genesis 9:18—27 (the subjugation of the descendants of Ham), and remember neither Jesus nor Paul advocated or started an anti-slave movement. Personally, I believe there will come a time in the future when we'll look back on the church's attitude to women with equal horror and regret.

Surely when we look at Scripture as a whole we see a different perspective? It was never in God's heart to see the domination of one race, class or sex by another. These injustices came about as the result of sin and sin alone. Now, in God's word, we see slavery in a new light, lifted to a higher plane. We can actually choose to be servants or slaves of the Lord, captivated and chained by love. It's my opinion that those who, perhaps quite sincerely, promote their belief that leadership should be entirely male, will stand embarrassed before the throne of grace along with those good men who were equally convinced that God's word endorsed their use of slaves. This may be a subjective and impassioned plea, but I'm sure it is nonetheless valid, especially in the light of so much divergence of biblical interpretation among evangelical scholars. However, I will look more closely at what the Bible does say elsewhere in my book, I don't want to dodge the issue.

I trust you are beginning to understand how God views women? Psalm 139 assures me that I was no divine blunder. When God made me he didn't blink, or turn aside for a moment to sneeze and 'whoops', there was another woman. When Father dealt with Abram he didn't only give him a new name, Abraham, he gave Sarai a new name also, Sarah, and told her she would be the mother of nations (Gen 17:15). Sarah was given her vision directly from God, she didn't just catch it from Abraham. Later when Abraham sent out his servant Eleazer to find a wife for his son Isaac, Rebekah didn't have to be persuaded or abducted, she came willingly as a bride. She too had her own relationship with God.

No, God is not sexist in his behaviour, although sometimes he has appeared to be that way to me. For example, in Numbers 12 there is obviously a split here in the leadership team as Aaron and Miriam are both moaning about Moses. God called them before him and his anger burned against them and came around them like a cloud. Quite a picture, God's wrath must have been a tangible, visible thing for the Bible to say, 'It was like a cloud.' When the cloud lifted from them both it was Miriam who was left with leprosy. 'That doesn't seem fair,' I cried when I read it. 'Why Miriam? The cloud was around both of them.' Well, to begin with, whoever said God was fair? He does what is right. He will not conform to our standards of fairness. It may not be fair that my hair is straight and yours curly, but that's the way God made it. God wasn't fair when he sent his only Son to die for my sins. It wasn't very fair, but thank you, Jesus, and thank you, Father, that you knew what you were doing.

This story of Aaron and Miriam troubled me for ages. The people I asked about it had really not looked at it from the woman's angle at all, and that's not surprising really as none of them were women. I put my puzzlement on hold for a long while and in the meantime a variety of people mentioned different aspects of the occasion. I was beginning to build up a picture of this incident. Suddenly, for me, the whole thing came into focus. I saw it, not as a sexist act on God's part, but as a very salutary lesson to the whole of Israel.

Miriam had leprosy for one week. She spent that time outside the camp and everyone waited to see the outcome. Leprosy could not be tolerated, it was an infectious disease. No amount of sacrifice or repentance would allow a leper to be received back into society. Only outright healing was acceptable. This was how seriously God looked upon their complaining. Perhaps there is a lesson here for us all. It was Aaron who instantly turned to Moses and, wondering at his own escape, pleaded for his sister. Moses turned to the Lord and the sentence was reduced to seven days. You see, Aaron was a priest and should he have had the leprosy, even though he was healed, the law said he could never be a priest again. He came within a hair's breadth of losing his right to continue in his office, but God was merciful and used Miriam to be the demonstration of his anger towards their sin. No, this was not an example of God being unfairly selective against a woman, but rather we see God's mercy being extended towards a man and also to his chosen people.

The incident does not reflect an image of a God who has one set of rules for women and another for men. Rather, it reveals a God who ministers correction in the way that is best in each individual circumstance. Hebrews 12:6 teaches us that God chastens, or puts right, those he loves. In this case he loved both Miriam and Aaron as well as all Israel. He also knew them intimately. He did not lash out as we do at times, leaving damage behind us, but provided the perfect act of discipline for everyone involved. Micah 6:1–4 clearly states that God counted Miriam as a part of the leadership team in spite of her failure, her leprosy and her sex. Later, Moses' own sin kept him out of the promised land, but in God's mercy he was there with Jesus on the Mount of Transfiguration.

God really loves us and always wants to include us in; male and female together we are his greatest creation, the top of the pile, la crème de la crème. God doesn't seem to worry too much about the sex of his servants. He simply looks into their hearts. He is willing to use us in ways which are fitted to the personalities and abilities which, after all, he gave us in the first place, didn't he?

7

What Do Women Feel About Themselves?

In discussing how women feel about themselves it would be impossible for me to cover all the variations of shades from black, through grey, to white. I realise that I am therefore, almost invariably, speaking in quite extreme terms. If you don't find yourself fitting in exactly with my description, add a little black or white to the mixture to make your particular shade of grey.

Women know exactly what they want, it's just that they aren't always quite sure just exactly what it is that they want! Yes, you really did read what you thought you read. It's not a misprint. For many of us this statement really does sum up how we feel. Often our knowing takes a very negative form. We are able to say exactly what we don't want, but find it hard to be straightforward and positive. For example, we don't want to be passed over in a discussion, but go ahead and ask if we have a contribution and we will probably answer 'No', even before we've thought about it. Any-way, thanks for asking! We also feel things deeply and are sometimes shocked by what we feel and so we tend to think that we must be wrong. When we do attempt to verbalise our concerns we constantly fall into the trap of trying to justify them. As we progress in our explanation, the look on our listener's face, our husband, boyfriend, father or leader, becomes more and more bemused as he understands less and less what it is that we are actually saying.

God has gifted me with an intuitive gift and frequently I feel things, usually very strongly. At times I cannot back up what I feel with facts. If I could the feeling would be superfluous. When this happens my male hearers are cross-eyed and totally at sea. Why are we inveigled into caricatures of one another by Satan? He forces us miles apart from those we love by pressing us to make demands of one another to communicate in a particular way. I have been learning, quite painfully at times, to believe in the gift which God has given me. I am also learning not to be pressurised into using gifts which he hasn't given to me. Actually, you'd think it would be much easier to keep quiet than share the things you feel, but nothing is further from the truth. When I have kept things to myself with my usual, unspoken excuse, 'I'm probably wrong,' I feel terrible. I know I have let both the Lord and myself down in failing to share what is often the prompting of the Holy Spirit. Now, immediately I get one of my feelings, I endeavour to say to those I'm sharing with, 'I may be very wrong, but I want you to know....' Then I'm prepared to leave it and the passage of time usually sorts out the rights and the wrongs of what I said. Time has its own way of resolving the truth about our feelings, prophecies, sermons, in fact all kinds of words we utter. If you do consistently get things right, you should gain the respect of your brothers and sisters and also their authority to speak more and more.

If only God had made a clean job of separating out his creation in the garden. All women would be intuitive and prophetic feelers and all men would be logical, authoritative and down-to-earth thinkers. Well, he didn't! If he had chosen to, he could have made two clearly-defined parcels: one of all the masculine attributes, the other of all the feminine attributes. However, the Lord didn't choose to make it that clear. He divided up the mix in his own way and left us to put it back together again. As we work and live in harmony, together we make a whole.

There are those who say that if God is only fully represented by male and female, then Jesus would have had to have been bisexual to have been a complete expression, but they have missed the point. It's not our sexuality that reflects God, for in the kingdom there is neither male nor female, nor ultimately even marriage. It is our attributes. The fullness of God was in Christ, of that I'm sure, but while God's stamp is on all of us, no one man or woman or even couple can contain all of God. He needs a whole nation of believers to reflect the glory of his Son. It is the completed church which will fully represent Christ, as he did God. We believers, all of us together, are the body of Christ and he needs the contribution each one of us has to make in order to be fully visible on earth.

When we begin to grasp the extent to which Satan has successfully undermined the relationship between men and women, we also begin to understand the depth of the internal struggle which goes on in each one of us. We realise how much we have been conditioned to think and feel as we have for hundreds of years and over countless generations. I was listening to the radio recently and a young woman of about eighteen or so was speaking about the opposition she was experiencing and having to cope with at school. As I remember her story, she had been to an all girls' school. She had taken 'O' levels and done extremely well and had therefore decided to go ahead with 'A' levels. This called for a change from the girls' school to a sixth form college where, for the first time, she had boys in the classroom with her.

From day one she was under fire. You see she wasn't taking arts subjects, such as English literature, art, cookery or needlework, she was taking science subjects like physics, maths and chemistry. She reeled under the onslaught of remarks ranging from, 'You'll never catch a husband with that lot,' to, 'Will your poor little brain stand it?' This stopped her in her tracks. Until this point in time she had received only encouragement academically, but she now found herself confused by all that was happening to her. She was talking about the feelings which flooded into her. Feelings of fear and insecurity which previously she hadn't been aware of. I'm sorry to say I don't know the end of the story. I was listening to the programme in the car and at that moment I lost the station. But here was another example of how prejudices are acted out, passed on and perpetuated. I did pray that she wouldn't resign her God-given gifts of logic and reason because of the male chauvinism she met in the classroom. The conditioning starts young, doesn't it? Actually it's unusual for a girl to survive as long as she did.

It's true, women do seem to be in a muddle about themselves and their worth as human beings. It's amazing how some women stay with, care for, make love to and carry the children of men who beat them up, pour scalding water on them, tug handfuls of hair from their heads and perhaps even break their jaws. But they do it, and I believe at rock bottom the reason they stay in these appalling circumstances is their own feeling of worthlessness and low self-esteem. When you talk to such women they speak in terms of, 'Who else would have me and my children?'

Refuges for battered women have recently been in

the news. The feeling still seems to persist that a man beating his woman is somehow permissible. It's called a 'domestic crisis'. If this type of violence were to happen between two strangers, in all probability one would end up in jail, but certainly not if the protagonists are married or co-habiting. Pioneer Erin Prizzey opened the first refuge for women in the world in Chiswick during 1972, and some minor legislation has been passed since then to protect women. This is, as far as I can find out, a non-Christian organisation. We don't have anything like it in the church. You may be saying that we don't need it. Well, I'm not sure about that. First, we should not only be concerned about the 'in crowd' and, secondly, in counselling I know first-hand that Christians are not exempt from these particular problems. Shocking as it may be, unless we help the men to shake free from the pressure of believing in their divine right to rule with a rod of iron if they choose, we are not going to see any substantial changes. Women too must be delivered from believing they are so worthless, and they must learn not to take passively all that is meted out to them in this way.

The evils of our society are coming much more to the surface these days. We are disgusted by the news of rape, incest, child abuse, woman beating and AIDS all around us. As Christians we must not close our eyes to these things and believe that the church is entirely free from them. This would, indeed, be burying our heads in the sand. Unless we give Satan his marching orders and start taking back ground in the church to which he has gained access, we will have no power to bring about lasting changes in the lives of needy people in the world.

Women in the world need to be delivered from the twisted mirrors they spend so much time gazing into. These mirrors are distorting, satanic inventions. They show women that they are not the correct shape,

weight, colour or sex, to name but a few of the lies
reflected back to us. The prettiest girl has eyes too small
or mouth too large. The slimmest figure is too long in
the waist or too short in the leg. Age is to be feared, as
are lines on the face, and a sag in the breast can be the
forerunner of a nervous breakdown.

It's all so different for women in the church. Or is it?
More often than not it's a woman's overwhelming need
and feeling of rejection and worthlessness which causes
her to turn to Christ. He will accept her just as she is,
but somehow she finds it so hard to believe. It's too
good to be true. She reads that we are all one in Christ,
but it seems to her that in the church structures, some
are more 'one' than others. In the main, preaching,
teaching and working for God comes over as being an
extremely male-orientated occupation, with women
gaining recognition through being married and having
children. I asked two respected men I know how they
view this particular issue in relation to the Scriptures.
One answered me with, 'Well, there you are, Christine.
If the Bible is heavily masculine there must be something in it!' The second man's answer was, 'Frequently,
the problem is in the choice of words used by the
translator. The male word is often used when a common or collective word is needed. There are few of these
available and most of the translators lived in an
extremely male-dominated culture anyway. With the
passage of time the words have become aggressively
male.'

Translators even argue about the gender of names,
just in case a female name comes through and blows to
smithereens their ideas and structures. Certainly, even
I understand that if we were to take all the occasions
when the Bible refers to 'men' and 'brethren' as being
men only, lots of beautiful promises would be lost to
women altogether. I can find five such references

between verses 10 and 17 of 1 John 3 alone. I'm not suggesting that we change the text, only that we should read it with new eyes.

Many of the books I have read in my endeavour to understand myself, haven't helped me very much to resolve my problems. One type of book urges me, as a married woman, to reduce all my problems to a time and motion study. The major content deals with when and how to do my chores, although it does give advice on sexual matters. Wear no underclothes, or wear nothing at all, for if I get my sexual act together, I could reduce my male to a quivering heap of desire, ready to get his cheque book out for anything I could possibly want. Well, I want to be free to take my clothes off at the appropriate moment, but not as a means to an end. I'll do it because that's a joy between my husband and me. Those tactics wouldn't work for me anyway as John would see through me like a pane of glass. Besides, we have a joint account and I have my own credit cards! I don't want to gain advantage by sexual means. It's a free gift from the Lord; let's keep it that way.

Another type of book leans heavily towards rigid structure of the pyramidic kind, with hubby at the top and the family pets at the bottom. Although holding dear the aspect of the husband in the marriage retaining authority, my understanding of the biblical view is that he and his wife are partners. He certainly does not retire to his study and from that holy place get the 'revelation' so that he can come back with all the decisions made. Then 'wifey' just smiles sweetly and agrees while he doles them out to the rest of the family, including the dog. How do such men do it? Why doesn't the Lord speak to us all like that?

It seems to me that I must be extremely perverse (no cries of 'hear, hear' please), but even some of the recent books written about 'women from the Bible' don't do anything for me. They leave me feeling cheated and bemused. Can I be so out of step, I ask myself? Are we reading the same Bible? These books, mostly written by women for women, use women in the Bible as examples. Fair enough, but must they always be the same ones? Usually they are the ones who got it wrong like Michal, David's wife who sneered at his dancing, or Naomi who was filled with bitterness, or Job's wife who urged her husband to curse God and die, or Lot's wife who glanced over her shoulder and became a pillar of salt. We are told of their weaknesses and God's judgements upon them and how we must watch to see that we are not found wanting in the same way. The need for silence, modesty, submission and humility are constantly rehearsed, all of which is only one side of a clearly two-sided coin. What about Jael, Esther, Deborah, Ruth, Abigail, Rahab, Lydia, Priscilla, Phoebe and a host of others from which we can conjure up a very different picture of fortitude, faith, aggression and passion? Women tend to dwell upon their failures and faults, while men tend to ignore theirs on the whole. How many sermons have you heard about Shimei, the guy who cursed David, or Nabal, Korah, Judas or Simon the sorcerer? Women tend to see their failures as disqualifying them, whereas men are inclined to view their weaknesses as almost macho. We see this particularly in our attitudes towards sexual exploitation: women feel defiled, men feel mature. Somehow, without throwing out the need to face our weaknesses, we must redress the balance and encourage our ladies far more than we have in the past to become warriors for the kingdom and its cause.

All in all we women do feel quite muddled as to our identity, function and usefulness in the church. Making tea and sandwiches, arranging the flowers and teaching Sunday school are all, needless to say, terrific things to do for those gifted in these areas, but suppose you have other gifts? Perhaps your tea is like paint stripper, your sandwiches doorsteps, your flowers die on you, and you find it difficult to understand the needs of children at all. Where is your place? Are you to be a woman just filling a pew?

It is always difficult for anyone holding power to relinquish any of it to another. Prime Ministers don't resign with ease. Monarchs don't abdicate without persuasion. Top executives would rather die in harness than resign. Leaders in the church are no exception. Tragically most do not see their task as making room for their disciples or doing themselves out of a job. Their fulfilment is not to see others released and functioning, but their security comes in being more and more needed. If women are to take their place in the church properly, we will need a revolution in the thinking of our men. Without losing their dignity or the true leadership God has given, they will need to open up the closed ranks to make a little room to let the women in.

We need to see a few spaces created which may take a little time to fill, but once we have begun I believe God will enable us to stand in rank side by side. When thinking of this, Ezekiel's vision in chapter 37 verses 1–14 came to mind. First the bones were knit together in order making the skeleton, then the skin and flesh were laid on the bones and finally the breath of God was breathed into the bodies. Only when each bone was in place could God's plan move forward. His plan is for an army, an army of ordinary people, men and women doing extraordinary things together under the authority of their Lord and Master. The same Spirit which raised Christ from the dead, also quickens his army to engage in the final battle which will utterly defeat the Enemy and bring back the King.

8

Boundaries and Barriers

There is, for me, a vast difference between boundaries and barriers and I trust that by the end of this chapter you will see the difference for yourselves. In my terms, boundaries are God-given, whereas barriers have been wrongly erected to obstruct us. The one is good, the other is evil. In Bible times, boundaries were often marked by single stones, at the corners of a field for example, rather than by walls or fences. The stones were a reminder of ownership, rather than barriers making 'no go' areas. The single stones became high walls as greed, fear and violence increased in the world.

Boundaries are necessary and beneficial, especially once we know where they should be and what they are for. My skin is a boundary. One of its functions is to keep the rest of my body in place. Without it I would be in a sorry state, unacceptable at the dinner table or anywhere else for that matter. Another boundary is my sexuality. A woman can give birth to a baby, a man cannot. Marriage comes into this category, as it was intended to be the context in which one man and one woman could relate physically together in sexual union. One's gifts and abilities were also designed to function within their boundaries. One realm where there are very clear guidelines for the children of God, is their relationship to Satan and all his works. Let's look at one or two scriptures which show us where the Lord draws some of his boundary lines.

Deuteronomy 18:10 says, 'Let no-one be found among you who sacrifices his son or daughter in the fire, who practises divination or sorcery, interprets omens, engages in witchcraft, or casts spells, or who is a medium or spiritist or who consults the dead. Anyone who does these things is detestable to the Lord.' Most of us would agree with and accept these boundary lines. What about the first statement, however? Do we disregard this as not relevant to today? Think again! What happens to the millions of aborted babies? Yes, these sons and daughters are sacrificed in the fire. Sobering thought, isn't it?

Then in Leviticus 20:13 we read: 'If a man lies with a man as one lies with a woman, both of them have done what is detestable.' Romans 12:3, 6 tells us: 'Do not think of yourself more highly than you ought, but rather think of yourself with sober judgement in accordance with the measure of faith God has given you.... We have different gifts, according to the grace given us.' Finally, back to Deuteronomy: 'Cursed is the man who moves his neighbour's boundary stone' (27:17).

It's pretty obvious from these words that God is a God of order and his boundaries are given to us for our security. Each of us needs to discover them for ourselves and we must not move them around, either in our own lives or the lives of others.

Barriers, on the other hand, are a very different matter. They should never have been put there in the first place. They have been raised directly by the Enemy, or he has manoeuvered us into erecting them ourselves. His intention is to cripple or imprison us and so keep us from serving God, or even to enlist us into his own service. Some barriers become obvious as we get to know God better. Others have been subtly introduced deep into our very beings through family, culture or religious conditioning. It is our responsibility to uncover and dismantle these structures so that we may function freely in our relationship with Jesus. In the next few paragraphs I should like to examine some of these barriers. First, those which particularly relate to women.

'Women were made to be married.' It may sound right, but what a terrible stumbling block to women who feel called by God to serve him in the single state. 'A woman's place is in the home!' Many women have stifled godly desires and even suffered nervous breakdowns as they have struggled with this pressure. 'Babies and children are the responsibility of women!' This is more often than not the case, but there are women who don't relate to young children at all well and are out of place in that role. Equally, there are many men who love children and should be released to be involved in the task of raising and training them. 'Women are best equipped for housework and cooking!' If this is really true, how is it that men claim they are the best chefs in the world, but are rarely found in the family kitchen?

There are women who live their lives in misery and failure because they can't achieve the required standards in home management. It's not that they haven't tried. Perhaps they were made for other things. A case in point here is Elizabeth Fry. She, apparently, was a very bad manager of her home and children, so much so that finally her children were taken on by her relatives. It was at this point that her ministry into prisons began. She was a prison visitor and stepped into situations of squalor and degredation such as we would find difficult to imagine. She was not a domestic woman, but one on fire for God. It is difficult to judge history, as we rarely have all the facts, but suffice it to say that Elizabeth Fry brought hope to many. Some of those whom she comforted were approaching the scaffold, others were being transported for their crimes. Who knows, perhaps she was forced into marriage by the pressures of her day and age?

'Women are not logical!' Rational-minded women may feel unfeminine and gauche because of this sweeping generalisation. It is also said that women are emotional and therefore they cannot handle authority! Along the same lines it could be argued that because men fight shy of responsibility they cannot be trusted to lead! Anyway, in lots of churches and fellowships the level of governmental discipline is so low that it could be carried out by a sanctified Koala bear, let alone a woman. These are but a few of the barriers which hem us in and prevent us from being the women God made us to be.

Equally, there are ungodly restrictions which determine how men should live their lives. Bachelors are either doomed to forgetfulness and untidiness or the social whirl of wine, women and song. Single men are pressed to take pride in their macho image, even though they may actually have a real creative streak or a desire to make a home.

'Men must work to support their families!' In today's climate of unemployment some fellows struggle in mental anguish feeling unmanned at their lack of a job when, for some, it would be possible for their wives to find employment. 'Men are not interested in babies!' What a divisive lie this can be for fathers right at the start of their family life. There must be innumerable men who need healing from this deception. 'Carpentry, decorating and car maintenance are the male domain and men should also look after the finance!' Has anyone bothered to find out how many men consider themselves to be substandard because they are hopelessly impractical or useless at budgeting? 'Men are not emotional or intuitive!' In a sentence, many sensitive guys are robbed of their prophetic or artistic gifts and never function because they have been limited by this kind of pigeon-holing.

'Neither men nor boys should cry!' I remember so clearly the day I recognised the conditioning my son was receiving in this area. We were in the casualty department of the local hospital, a place well-known to many mothers and children. On one occasion I was asked if I wanted a season ticket! The nurse was going through the usual patter with my small, sobbing boy with his broken arm. 'Now then, be a brave man. Stop crying. Big men don't cry!'

I suddenly recognised the lie. 'Darling, if it hurts you cry,' I found myself saying. 'If you go over the top I shall smack you, but when you are in pain you have every reason to cry.'

This phrase: 'A real man,' is whispered by the Enemy over and over again. 'A *real* man never shows fear or love,' is another example.

'Men should always take the lead!' Such thinking can cause some men to be incredibly overstretched and out of their depth, sometimes resorting to a false authority in an endeavour to maintain an appearance of being in control.

How Satan has deceived us with his grossly-exaggerated typecasting. He has taken elements of truth and made a caricature which is no more the reality than saying that men and women must always be exactly the same. Growing numbers of women in the world are turning to militancy, demanding that all barriers and boundaries must go. They press far beyond the reasonable and even seek to destroy those God-given limitations which are there for our protection. They have been hurt by the many wrongs, but have now become obsessed with a mission to abolish all distinctions. They despise any man who doesn't support their crusade and some despise all men. I do understand the desperate pain behind their aggression, but I cannot identify with their actions or their willingness to use almost any means to achieve their ends. This is not God's way.

Of course, we must work for justice. Equal work deserves equal pay, regardless of colour, class or sex, but equality itself is not the goal. My quest is for the right to be unique. Our heavenly Father has never been into mass-production, or even limited editions. He creates 'one offs' all the time. Sadly, we in the church have been dragging our heels when we should have been setting the pace. Satan has done a marvellous job of raising these barriers between men and women. He has done it unseen and unnoticed. He carefully laid the trap and we walked right on in. He built the walls and then supplied both factions with guns and ammunition. We have ignored or forgotten his part in all this and laid the blame on one another.

So great is the damage and build-up of venom in some feminists, that they want to do away with any kind of dependence on men altogether. They have believed the father of lies, who has told them that they don't need men at all. What horrors await them down this pathway; what terrible suffering and pain as they bathe themselves in bitterness and hatred? Who is to stop them and who can help?

Surely Satan's plan for women has reached its climax in the Western world? A woman can now acquire the same education as a man; she can earn as much as a man; she has the same career opportunities as a man.

Great! But she can also choose another woman as her sexual partner; she can go to a sperm bank for her baby; she can choose to demonstrate that fathers are totally unnecessary in this brave new world. What price this freedom when it leads you steadily away from God and closer to hell? We in the church must demonstrate through love, peace and fearlessness that there is another way.

The whole church, not just some women or certain enlightened men, must provide a guiding light in the great darkness which engulfs so many of our fellow human beings. Even while we are finding full agreement among ourselves we can show Christ's love to one another and to those outside the fold. We must be humble and honest about the inconsistencies in our thinking and actions. How is it that we allow a fine Christian woman to carry a successful executive position in business for years, and yet deny her the right to use those same abilities in the church? How we can encourage women to work among dangerous tribes and in primitive places and yet forbid those same women any authority in even the smallest fellowship meeting at home, is beyond me. We must begin to see the river of God's Spirit producing the same quality of life as it runs through every turn of our experience. Our work, homes and church life must stand up to scrutiny and wherever the world's microscope is turned on the people of God, it must find Christ shining through. The world must see us rejoicing together as the barriers of centuries come crashing down. It will watch amazed as we yield to the tremendous freedom Jesus gives and to the loving limitations he places, not only upon women, but every disciple of his, both male and female.

Well, I've certainly taken the liberty to be black and white here to make my point. I did warn you at the start that I would be. However, I do want to add a small note of caution. When you turn down a road and are confronted by one of those red and white barriers carrying a notice which says: 'Danger no entry!' your first reaction should be to take note. To drive on rebelliously could mean that you and your vehicle end up at the bottom of a deep hole. Sometimes Father does take emergency action in our lives for our safety and well-being. For example, just recently after major surgery, I found one of my side roads blocked. I was told quite clearly no exercise for six months. That put the lid on my dancing as a way of priasing the Lord. I would have been very foolish to ignore this warning without specific permission from Father.

For some of you such a limitation would have been no great problem—in fact getting you to move at all would be a major miracle. For me, no dancing was very hard, but thank God the restriction was only for a season. It would have been quite possible for me to have accepted the temporary barrier as permanent after the six months were up. I could have allowed habit or fear to have taken over and the Enemy would then have gained ground in my life. So stop the car every now and again and peep over the barrier to see how the work is progressing. If it is slow or has stopped altogether, nip round to your local government office and make a few personal enquiries. You may find things aren't quite what they seem to be and a complaint to the correct department will open things up again.

Sometimes temporary barriers have been raised in our lives by our brothers and sisters in the church, because we need moral discipline for one reason or another. This may be for our benefit and correction, ministered with the very best intentions. Those of us responsible for such discipline, and on the whole we're pretty slack to admonish one another in this way, should remember that the purpose is always remedial.

When we see the response of repentance and obedience, we must be willing to take the barriers down and restore freedom once again. Just like the plaster cast on a broken leg, or the diet for an ulcer sufferer, when healing comes normality can be restored. If we don't remove the restrictions the treatment can become a lasting feature which wrongly limits our life and function.

In all this, it's my desire to see people set free from the cages which have been so carefully constructed by our adversary. One of my aims is to help us dispel the fog which confuses our discernment. I long that we will be able to distinguish between the boundaries which have been lovingly laid out by our Father, and the barriers which have been cunningly designed by the Devil. We need to shake off the fears which keep us from prayerfully exploring the desires of our hearts. Only then will we discover whether or not the restrictions were put there by the Holy Spirit. We may make mistakes, but that is not the end of the world. There is always forgiveness from Father. There may be criticism and misunderstanding, but we can also forgive one another. Of one thing I'm absolutely sure: we must begin to move forward together into this amazing field of discovery. We must care for one another as we go, watching out for one another and releasing one another into all that has been planned for us as men and women of God.

9

Married or Single?

For our Christian single people, it must seem that recently we have been majoring overmuch on marriage. I offer no excuses, we have! Marriage and the family are under attack and in many cases they are in total disarray. Never has it been so simple to obtain a divorce, nor so widely accepted that marriage is outdated and unnecessary. We have been redressing the balance and bringing the spotlight of God's love into the area of this most basic of relationships: the sexual. We do, however, need to take a look at the single state and consider it as being of the utmost importance to what God is doing in the church today.

What does God have in mind for single people then? Have they missed the boat if they are single? Or have we missed it if we are married? As with all other aspects of our lives I believe the answer is found in God's particular gifting and calling for each individual. This really means that there should be no conflict between these two states, but an acceptance of one another's calling and circumstances. We should also expect active support and encouragement for the single from the married and vice versa. Here again we discover that

Satan has been very busy. He has successfully planted confusion, conflict, jealousy, spite and rejection in our hearts towards one another.

Marriage should be a miniature working model of the relationship Christ longs to have with his church. When this has truly been written in our hearts, then the world will be able to look at our marriages and see spiritual reality at work. When a woman submits herself to her husband and there is order and harmony in the home, this will speak oceans into the rat-race of life which is most people's experience. When a man loves a woman in such a way that he would willingly sacrifice himself to see his wife living her life to the full, the world may not understand, but they will certainly be aware that there is something missing from their own relationships. In the same way, when people choose to be single because they find it a better way to serve Christ, in their unselfishness we will catch a glimpse of Jesus, who denied himself those simple rights in order to serve us.

In choosing to be married, I have voluntarily taken on the boundary of one man, and he has also taken on the boundary of one woman. Neither of us is any longer free to pursue God's calling on our lives without reference to the other. Let me give you an example. I have some friends who have been married now for quite a few years. The story begins before they married. The girl felt that God had called her to India and that one day she would go there. In the meantime she fell in love. Her man didn't have that same call on his life. He felt they should stay and work for the Lord just where they were on the east side of London. So with this understanding they married and settled down. She never lost her call to India, but she understood that if it truly came from God it was his responsibility to work it out. The years passed and the couple were close to retirement age. The leader of their church went to India and on his return felt that the greatest help they could give their brothers and sisters in that part of the world, was to assist in the setting up of a printing press of their own. Who were they to send to oversee this important task? It would need to be someone who knew the job and could iron out any difficulties. Guess who was the printer? You're right of course, it was the husband. Here they are, many years later, on their way to India. God was able to work it all out in history. He never puts boundary lines in our lives to frustrate us, but to help us become the people he wants us to be.

A man who is called to an itinerate ministry must consider the new boundary line in his life once he is married. He can no longer just shoot off all over the world at the drop of a hat. He must consult his bride. He must bring her and her needs into consideration. Marriage changes things! It is so important that before a couple plunge headlong into marriage they should together count the cost and have worked out some sort of game plan or understanding. Do they both want children? If not, who is going to take precautionary action? If they do have children and they're both involved in the work of the church, who will care for them during those first vital months and years? If the woman in this potential partnership would like to carry on with her responsibilities, how will her man feel about it? Will he cope or should she be willing to lay down her work so that the relationship can continue on into marriage and family? These same questions will also apply if the man has responsibilities.

We do need to start by asking the correct questions and, even more important, find the right answers. Married people, or those looking towards marriage, are not alone in their need for clarity. Single folk must also face up to the pressures which may come their way.

Historically, being a single woman has so often

caused its own difficulties, with raised eyebrows and question marks. In the past, being alone could lead to all sorts of trouble and accusations. It was not unknown for a whisper to sweep round a village, 'She's a witch!' Many women were adept at home medicine, knowing which plants, roots and leaves could be used to help different ailments. It took only a short step in the imagination for some superstitious or religious soul to leap from medicine to incantation; from helping a mother whose child had a bad cough, to cows dying in a meadow after 'that woman' had passed by. To be single was questionable. Sometimes, in order to avoid such trouble, particularly in a large family where the father could not raise another daughter's dowry, the single girl was pressed into becoming a nun. Marriage was the goal for every woman. Failing this she was a subject for speculation which caused her great distress.

In our modern society, marriage is purposefully pushed aside as being no sort of answer at all. But to be alone can still be questionable. You don't have to be married to acquire status, but your body needs sex, so live with someone. Perhaps you don't particularly care for male company. That's fine, choose another girl as your partner. But to live entirely alone from choice, that's weird!

Some London boroughs introduced into their schools a book which was used to teach reading to infants. It showed a small girl living at home with her daddy and his boyfriend. The three of them have breakfast in bed together, Mummy comes to visit, and the acceptability of homosexual behaviour is explained and applauded. I was horrified at just how fast Satan is leading people along the road to destruction. This particular book has now been withdrawn, because of the pressure that was brought to bear at both parental and ministerial levels. Perhaps we should all take care to find out what books are being used to teach our children to read. In fact, make it a practice to take a look at the books children are being encouraged to read at every level. Marriage, the family and the individual are certainly under attack. Our adversary is committed to leading us as far away from God's plan as he possibly can.

In the church we are also guilty of maligning the role of single Christians. With so much emphasis on marriage we have neglected to encourage those who are single by choice. Without realising it we put pressure on them by our innuendos or silences. We do need to repent of a preoccupation with family life which at times has left our single folk feeling confused as to their worth and, on occasions, lonely and left out.

In the Bible we read Paul's statement that it is better to be single than married. For those who see his references to women as male chauvinistic and rigid, with their sphere of activity curtailed drastically to the home and marriage, perhaps now is the time to examine what Paul is saying in a new way. To remain single in order to work better for the Lord surely cannot refer only to men? This wouldn't make any sense as the women would need men to be married, then the men would no longer be single! Unless of course there were far more men than women, which seems unlikely when you consider the circumstances at that time: a Roman army of occupation, which would put down any insurrection brutally and probably with great loss of life; enslavement for domestic, army and entertainment purposes. I believe that Paul is referring to the freedom that any single person will experience if they devote themselves wholly to God. There is no boundary of marriage or children here to hold them back in any way.

But there is often confusion and muddled thinking like this when we interpret Scripture because we come with pre-conditioning. The same applies to the idea that all women should be submissive to all men. Invariably when the Bible speaks of women submitting to men it is in the context of marriage. Frequently the word 'man' would be more accurately rendered 'husband', and 'woman', 'wife'. The thought that all females should submit to all males is not to be found in Scripture. At best we can argue that all wives should be in submission to their husbands and that all women in the church should have a right attitude to the leadership. The latter is also true for men. They too should have respect for the leaders appointed in the church. On a number of occasions I have been horrified to see young, immature men dominating, not only their girlfriends, but also older women more experienced than themselves. This is not God's way.

Experience has led me to value single people enormously. My own family would be the poorer without their input over the years. Just to give you one example: some time ago three single people in our church came to John and me with a proposition. They had seen the pressure that I was under running a home for the family, now almost adult. I was involved in the leadership of the fellowship and also travelling in ministry more and more. In the midst of all this activity I was rapidly coming to the conclusion that something had to go from my schedule. These three young people offered to serve me. Two of them would continue to work in their present jobs, while the third, a girl, would leave her employment and work for me full-time in the home. That took my breath away, as you can well imagine, but they hadn't finished. The two working wanted to support the third totally. Together they would pay her a salary and her house-keeping as all three would live in with us. Not only a willing servant, but a paid one into the bargain. The year they gave me was truly a blessing, and took us from one phase of family life and ministry through into another.

I could relate many other experiences and examples in which single people have served and led in both our family and fellowship life. There is a wide world out there waiting for the release of such willing and able people to reach out in a multiplicity of ways, in church work, in business, in health, in education, in the arts, in politics. Indeed there are tremendous opportunities at all levels of life, both here in the UK and overseas, for single people who are called by God and devoted to his will.

We do need to lift the profile of the single people in our churches. More and more they must find out from God their particular calling, whether at home or abroad, in the church or family, but certainly to the glory of God. If we are to treat seriously what the Bible says, we must ask God to change the attitudes of many quite radically. Maybe then we will actively encourage some people to remain single. Our singles have far more to offer in the family and in the life of the church than babysitting and ironing for the women, or decorating and car repairs for the men, important though these things are. We have much ground to reclaim and many battles to fight, so let's begin to build married and single men and women together as a mighty fighting force for our God and his kingdom.

IO

A Lament for the Unsung Heroines

When all the arguments are over; when all the pros and cons have been weighed; when all the decisions have been made; when all has been said and done; there still remains a company of women unsung, unrewarded and often forgotten. In my opinion these ladies are the circulatory system that keeps many churches alive and functioning. Numbers of them have been treated terribly, but at best they have been taken for granted and given no real thought, love or understanding. Due primarily to our muddled thinking in the church we have made demands on their time, their gifts, their abilities, their families, their homes, their food and drink and their money, with little or no concern or recognition offered in return. More often than not we have failed to take into consideration the needs or feelings of the women themselves. In other words they go with their husband's job. I am referring to that army of oft-times misguided heroines married to ministers and full-time Christian workers.

Have you ever had one of those fun photographs taken at a fair-ground, or the seaside? You know the ones I mean? There is a piece of scenery with a number of characters painted on it. Perhaps a Spanish scene, or an old-fashioned wedding or swimming party. All the figures have holes where the faces should be. The idea is that you stand behind the scene, push your head through a hole and have your picture taken wearing the flaming red frilly dress of the flamenco dancer, or the gown of an Edwardian bridesmaid and so on. None of the cardboard cut-outs are you, and you would probably be in desperate trouble if suddenly called upon to fulfil such a part. Many Christian women find themselves in a similar situation in real life. Here before them is this stereotyped role which they are required to fill. Their own shape, size or personality matters little. So much that is pre-conceived is expected from 'the Christian worker's wife' and if I possibly can, I want to bring their dilemma sharply into focus.

The problem is twofold. The first difficulty arises with the awesome little phrase 'full time'. This dreadful label somehow implies that something more is to be demanded of you now than was ever expected before. When you first welcomed Jesus into your life and made him Lord, he became a real person and called you to follow him. Actually that was when you took on full-time responsibilities. That was the moment when you became a full-time worker for God. The whole of your day was his, waking or sleeping; whatever your job or lack of one; whatever your gifts and capabilities; whatever your background or past; from the start you were fully God's, every moment of every day. But something happens to the way people view you when you take on the title 'full-time Christian worker'. All that is really meant is that you are now earning your living directly by the work of the gospel. Sadly, the people you serve begin to feel that you have become their property. There is a subtle shift of emphasis. What you gave freely before is now their right because you're being paid, albeit sometimes very little. The second problem is that as the 'wife' you must fill the cut-out shape already designed for you, regardless of whether you really fit or not. In fact, if you have no desire to toe the line you may be considered unspiritual and unsubmissive. If you do play the required role, you are destined to become part of the decor. Let us examine some of the pressures put on women who find themselves in this kind of position.

When Christians marry, the husband is called upon by Scripture to leave his parents, cleave to his wife and they both become one flesh. In the church we frequently take this unity one stage further, and add the unspoken demand that there must also be one call on both lives. I want to say clearly that there is one call on our lives, and that call is to be followers of Jesus and doers of his will. But we do sometimes seem to get these weird ideas of how God wants us to live. We have only one life and the whole of it should be lived to the glory of God, whether we are doctors, company directors, housewives, secretaries, school teachers, dustmen, shop assistants, youth leaders, pastors, job hunters or whatever. All of us should know that we are called by God to do what we are doing. Our walk through each day should be one continuous stream, filled with the life of God. Wherever and whenever we are touched by others they should find Jesus on, or just below, the surface.

I love the story of Enoch in Genesis 5:18–24. When Enoch had lived sixty-five years, he became the father of Methuselah. After the birth of his first child, Enoch walked with God for another 300 years and had other sons and daughters. Altogether he lived 365 years. The story records that 'Enoch walked with God; then he was no more, because God took him away'. I call Enoch a 'was not'. He came to know God intimately in the course of an ordinary existence, simply by being married and having a family. He became so close to God that one day he just walked off the earth into his presence—in the words of the old translations, he 'was not'. The honest ones among us know full well that on that basis alone, it takes 365 years to perfect us! But Enoch walked and talked with God while living a normal life. To become a 'was not' like Enoch, the whole of our lives need to be filled with Jesus. Paul talks of a whole generation of ordinary people who overcome death and step right on into Father's eternal presence.

One call on our lives, then? Yes! Only one expression of that call because we are married? No, not necessarily. We don't expect this of wives in any other realm except those married to church leaders. Here we require almost the impossible. We ask one person, in this case the woman, to become an echo of, and completely involved in, the work of her husband, even though this may lead to frustration and feelings of low self-worth. Let us look at a few other examples and see the differences.

Take the doctor and his wife. He may be called out at night to deliver quads. He may spend hours studying to gain a new degree or fresh specialist knowledge. He may worry about a diagnosis and constantly work unsocial hours. Hopefully his wife encourages and supports him, but she is not expected to accompany him on the night calls. Neither does she clean the surgery, make his appointments or file his patients' notes for him. She may well be at home, pursuing the personal dreams and aspirations God has put in her heart.

Think about the bus driver and his wife. He may worry about driving during the rush hour or being mugged late at night. Perhaps he takes refresher driving tests and practises on a skid pad. But his wife is not expected to fill the bus with petrol, check that he has enough change for the fares, or ride on the bus at night with him, talking to him in case he should fall asleep.

On the other hand, look at the vicar or pastor and his lady. He has taken on the responsibility for a new church. He will concentrate on working with the church leaders, preaching and other important matters. She will be available to the leaders' wives, she will take the women's meetings and perhaps organise the play school and the mother and toddler group. She must draw up a rota for cleaning the church, and is maybe responsible for arranging the flowers and hospitality for visiting speakers. On top of all this there is the housework, cooking, shopping, school trips and checking the bank statements. She may well also make sure that the car is full of petrol and that the change box for parking meters actually has money in it. She will blend beautifully into the background and she will never feel, or at least show, that she is tired, dispirited, overworked, ill-used, unhappy or depressed. She will, however, happily listen to those who do feel that way and will offer good, sound advice, and she will always, but always, smile.

What a bleak picture I've painted. But for many of these ladies that's how it is. They are not asked to be themselves and find their own level in the new situation, but to fulfil someone else's idea of how they should be involved. Some are convinced that it is the only way open to them to serve God. A few fit very well into this role and truly find fulfilment. For the others, we must ask ourselves why we demand that they should relate to the church on the basis of their husband's job. We don't expect it of anyone else. Are we really saying that these women are so different? Are we saying that just because they are married to a leader, that equips them more than others? Or have we never really thought it through at all? Are we simply perpetuating a tradition that came from no one knows where?

To continue my reasoning, let me dig a little deeper and ask: Is it necessary for both partners in the kind of marriage we are talking about to have to respond together and agree about everything? If they differ, is this a disaster for both the marriage and ministry? Because they are married, do they have to have identical dreams, hopes and aspirations? For so long the standard answer has been 'yes', but I believe with the fresh wind of the Spirit which is now blowing in the church we are becoming more secure and open to new ways of thinking. Some are realising that different roles and callings within a marriage are not necessarily the same as divorce. Varieties of expression and service need not be diminishing to a marriage where each partner has a different emphasis. There is not only one way to skin a cat; there are several. Being together in your marriage, with differing burdens and ways of expressing yourselves, may be far more a picture of Christ and the church than we realise. A man way out in front making all the decisions and course adjustments with the woman following passively behind, like one of those horrendous nodding dogs you see in the backs of cars, is not what God had in mind when he conceived of marriage. Jesus wants a church which is gloriously united in its diversity, not terribly boring in its uniformity. Christian marriage should be a shadow of the relationship between Christ and his bride. It should be exciting and challenging to the world, helping it to understand the nature of that final union. To achieve this, husbands and wives will need to make sacrifices for one another. One of the things my husband is constantly pointing out to men in leadership, is that Christ laid down his life for his bride that she might be released into all that she was made for. Christian husbands are called to do the same, not because they are nagged or cajoled, but because the Holy Spirit leads them in that way.

What about the special pressures which come with this particular job? There is the fabric of the home: the chairs, cups and carpets which get well-used and worn, more so than in most other homes. There is the loneliness that can sweep over a woman with the feeling that there is no way through without letting her husband and the church down. Since he is the leader, who can she turn to when she feels he has made a questionable decision? Who can she talk to when she feels he is overworking? Whose shoulder can she cry on when he hasn't made love to her or shown any affection in a month? Can she join a keep-fit class without feeling guilty of neglecting her duties? How can she say she wants a holiday in a hotel where she won't have to do anything at all, when the money is needed to go to a conference, or repair the car? The answer to all these questions is the same as it is for anyone else: she needs friends.

We have somehow managed to dehumanise, not only the wives of leaders, but the men themselves and their children too. These folk are expected to be in the place where they always have the answer and are able to pour in the balm and bind up the hurting, but they too have needs from time to time. They also need people they can trust to keep their confidences and with whom they can share their hearts. Our leaders are not yet so perfect that they can do without such relationships within the body of Christ.

Do you know who are going to be the most difficult people to convince that changes need to take place? I believe it may well be the women themselves. For some there is a certain status in being married to a leader. Some may be flattered when offered opportunities to minister and use their gifts, even though it's just because of the one to whom they are married. Surely this is not a good enough reason to preserve the status quo? Others will not welcome change because of fear or because that's the way it's always been and they don't want their cosy nest disturbed. Perhaps for these my chapter title would have better read, 'A lament for the unsung and misguided heroines'!

My husband had one of his rare visions which I would like to share with you at this point. Being by his own admission a man with the gift of 'non-discernment', this picture in itself was something of a miracle. He actually saw it at a time when I had been ministering and had come under heavy fire from some of the women because of the things I had been saying. John saw a tapestry which a woman had been sewing all through her life. At times, when she had looked at the picture, it hadn't felt quite right to her in some way, but she had persevered and now it was almost finished. Just then someone came along and explained that she had two of the colours muddled. Where she had used green she should have used blue, and vice versa. The colours had been deliberately switched by an intruder at the very beginning. She was faced with a terrible decision. Should she bury her head in the sand and refuse to see the mistake, or should she forget the whole thing and put the tapestry away unfinished? Should she unpick the years of work and try to sew it over again, or should she go on with it in this new way?

Through the picture God had revealed the awful predicament which faces so many Christian women as they realise that the years of silence, restriction and passivity were not what the Lord had been asking of them. When it dawns upon them that much of the effort and pain came because of the substitution, bitterness crouches at the door, waiting to come in and defile them. They were deceived. The choice was yield or

rebel, and they never for a moment considered that
there may have been another way. The path of meek-
ness and humility which Jesus walked did not preclude
honesty. This route would have enabled them to maintain their conscience and dignity while continuing to
live in harmony through disagreement. But what now?
Has all the time and effort been totally wasted?

During the next decade many women will have to
answer these questions for themselves—not only about
their place and ministry, but on many other subjects
too. Myself, I'm quite determined to finish my particular tapestry. I'm certainly not going to unpick it or
allow bitterness to develop at the apparent waste of
time. For me there is only ever one thing to do when
you discover you got it wrong—repent! Give the whole
thing over to the Lord. He has a remarkable way of
bringing good out of evil when we truly bring him into
our troubles.

As we go on with God we will find him doing one of
his amazing miracles as he restores to us the years that
the locust has eaten. He will rearrange our tapestry and
bring beauty out of ashes. We are not alone. Over and
over again through the centuries men and women of
God have had to face fresh challenges from the Holy
Spirit which have turned their little worlds upside
down. They did not achieve their victories by ignoring
their problems or giving up. Let us join with the 'great
cloud of witnesses' who yielded in obedience to their
Lord and walked with him in triumph to the end.

II

Some Thoughts from the Old Testament

God's purposes and designs are clearly revealed in the Scriptures. There are plenty of signposts showing us the way. From Genesis we see that his original plan was for a man and woman to live together, love together and rule together in the garden. From this relationship they were to multiply and fill the earth with a whole race of people like themselves. During this idyllic existence and through obedience to God, it was intended that they should find and eat from the tree of life. In so doing they would become God's friends and live for ever. This plan, as we have already seen, was thwarted. Now the journey for mankind has to be back to the place God had always intended.

Man had been successfully separated from God. It was as though there were an uncrossable stretch of dangerous rapids between them. On one bank was man, on the other was God. Man, by his disobedience had created the problem, but only God could come up with an answer. God's answer in the first place was, as it were, to create stepping stones in the river; stones such as the law, animal sacrifice and the day of atonement. Such steps a brave man might attempt, but they were wet and slippery and many a good man ended up drowning and still we were unable to cross. This was no news to God, he was looking down the ages to one man who would make it over, leaving behind him not stepping stones but a bridge with a paved highway. Then there would be a safe crossing place for those who desired to follow him. I'm speaking, of course, about Jesus who has bridged the gulf of sin and death for us all.

However, to return to the Old Testament. As we have already seen from Genesis, God touched the woman's womb and she became unclean. During menstruation and childbirth a woman withdrew into the 'women only' world—quite a heavy burden when you consider that most women are affected by the former for seven days each month, and have the potential for the latter approximately once every year for a large part of their lives. A man was not to contact a woman during those times, or even anything that she might happen to touch. No wonder this regular withdrawal from everyday life had an effect on the men. Slowly but surely women were relegated to a place among the belongings of a man. The law which should have provided a stepping stone back to God became the very instrument of degradation for women.

Many women actually call their menstrual period 'the curse' and view it with distaste rather than as a sign in their bodies of the potential for life. I've heard all sorts of arguments as to whether or not women experienced this cycle before the Fall, or whether it started as a result of the Fall. I really don't know the answer and would probably end up more dizzy than I am now trying to work it out. Surely we can do no more than speculate?

Slowly, with the passage of time, Satan drove a wedge between the sexes. The law, reinforced by interpretation and tradition, pushed women into the seclusion of marriage and the home. It was a male world and males ruled. Circumcision, the sign of God's covenant, only applied to men. Men alone could be priests—in fact only Aaron's descendants. The priesthood was extremely exclusive. This apparent bias led to the attitude that only those who could participate were deemed competent to enter into covenant with God. A woman's status was therefore secondary as her very body seemed to imply it. This belief is still found among some leaders in the church today. Thank God that the New Testament makes it clear that circumcision of the flesh is of no avail—true circumcision being of the heart and not the body. In Christ the priesthood is open to all who believe. Women were once again allowed in, but God never actually locked women out.

At the time of Jesus' birth women had been brought so low that in the main they could neither read nor write. In Israel, God's promised land and people, the attitude towards women could be summed up in the words of a rabbi of that time: 'To teach a woman the Scripture is to teach her lechery!' What hope was there for women in that sort of atmosphere? We can perhaps begin to understand the erosion of self-esteem which took place within the female community as the purpose of the law was misrepresented and mixed with tradition by unspiritual men. Nevertheless, there were women who broke through under the Old Covenant and touched God.

In the story of Hannah and her desire for a son in 1 Samuel 1–2, we see a woman breaking through these inconsistencies. She was labouring under the stigma of having no child; she was considered to be a second-class citizen, and yet she was an individual before God. She sought the Lord for herself, she prayed, made her vow and even named the child herself when he arrived. She judged how long to stay at home with him, brought him at last to the temple, making her sacrifice and handing him over into Eli's care.

Likewise Jael, whose exploits are recorded in Judges 4–5, was also a lady who appeared to step out of line. Sisera, the commander of the Canaanite army, was on the run from Deborah. Jael saw him from her tent and called him inside, promising to hide him. He accepted the invitation and she gave him a drink of milk, hiding him under a pile of skins. Then, while he slept, she did a most unladylike thing. She went around to the back of the tent, found a tent peg and mallet and proceeded to drive the peg straight through his temple. By my count that was enticement, lying and murder. Deborah and Barak wrote a song about the incident and today she is one of God's heroines.

Even under the Old Covenant, God clearly placed signposts for us to follow. How about the marvellous lady in Proverbs 31? She accomplished things which bring tears to my eyes. I can just imagine the effect her achievements would have, even in this enlightened era of grace, on some of the men in the church today. When they heard of her exploits their eyebrows would disappear into their hair. She sold the house and bought a new one, no doubt making a good profit into the bargain. She embarked on a buying expedition on the other side of the channel and saved hard cash on all the duty-free bargains. She provided for the poor and needy of the locality and ruled the house well. 'Strong woman that!' would be the reaction of many men, glad that they weren't married to her. For plenty of women, even the thought of such activity would be enough to send them scuttling for cover. Strength in women is used as a club to beat us with. For some reason strength in a man is to be admired and encouraged, but in a woman it is undesirable and unacceptable. Our Proverbs lady was strong in the very best sense of the word. Surely, if I made a good profit on the house sale, didn't overspend but bought wisely from the cheapest sources, made sure that in my husband's new study everything was exactly where it had been in the old one, John would join the husband of that 'strong' lady in saying, 'I have full confidence in her.' We must stop being afraid of strength in women. If we give it to God he will temper it and use it. Weakness of the watery kind never accomplished anything worth while.

Time and time again the Scripture gives the lie to our mistaken belief in the patriarchal society as being God's eternal plumbline. The Song of Solomon shows us a picture of both male and female as being fully individual, without the dominance of one sex over the other. The lover entreats his bride and the story closes with them coming out of the wilderness with her leaning on his arm. The story of Abigail in 1 Samuel 25 does not exactly show us a picture of the meek, submissive woman we might expect. Abigail, meaning 'source of delight', is married to Nabal, which means 'fool'! Nabal owes a debt of gratitude to David. In the account David calls in the debt by asking for food and drink for himself and his men. Nabal refuses and Abigail, who hears of her husband's folly, quickly gathers together a picnic banquet which she takes to David. She implores him to accept the gift and forgive her husband for he was, as his name suggested, a fool. Strong actions and words for a quiet, submissive woman. But everyone's works will be judged in their context and outcome. David accepts her offering and explanation and refrains from destroying the men of Nabal's house. When Abigail returns home she tells her husband what she has done, and within ten days he is struck down by the Lord and dies. David hears of Nabal's death, marries Abigail and finally, when he comes to the throne, he makes her his queen. In the Old Testament the law seemed to stand as a guard on the presence of God, but men and women like David and Abigail who hungered after truth found that it had no power to keep them from God's grace. Hebrew society and tradition came to view the law as a restriction or a closed door rather than a challenge to receive mercy and thus rise above it by faith and trust in God.

Almost invariably it seems that we preach only about the mistakes women have made, seldom about their triumphs. Sarah is a case in point and Genesis 12–25 tells her story, interwoven with that of Abraham. The things I knew best about Sarah through the sermons I heard were that she laughed at God's promise of a son and that she was afraid. I discovered that there was quite a bit more to her than that, and when the time came the Lord gave her a new name as well as her husband. Oh, and by the way, Abraham was also guilty of laughing—check for yourself in verse 17 of chapter 17. The Bible clearly states that Sarah had passed the age of childbearing. Most of us understand what that means in terms of her body's cycle. There must have been a strong surge of faith within her as this change and reversal took place and she found herself pregnant. Sarah was around ninety years old at the time when, suddenly, that which was dead came alive again and God's promise became a reality. In our society the doctor is deeply concerned for a first-time mother at thirty-five years old, let alone ninety! It would be interesting to know how the women around her coped. The midwives must have been in a flat spin, but Sarah was a woman of faith just as Abraham was a man of faith and she also received promises from her God.

Isn't it clear to you by now that God is less concerned about us getting things 'dead right' than he is about our heart attitude? When we say, 'Use me, Lord,' he looks into our hearts, then at our gifts and our abilities, and uses us as he sees fit. This comes across beautifully in the Book of Esther. The two women in the story have such a lot to teach us about attitudes and about God's desire to use an individual to bring his blessing to the multitudes.

Vashti, the reigning Queen at the beginning of the story, is obviously very beautiful and used to the affairs of high estate. She was giving a banquet for the cream of society among the women of the Medes and Persians. The King sent for her from his banqueting palace with the men and she publicly refused to come. This was the response of a very self-assured lady, secure in her position and power alongside the King. She certainly wasn't fearful of the consequences when she sent back her answer 'No!' My own feeling is that Vashti had found security in her position, her beauty and the love of the King. The situation was akin to Israel's relationship with God when at times she took the Lord for granted. However, Vashti erred in her judgement, she overstepped the line and she fell. She was no longer welcome in the King's presence. Esther became her replacement and did not put her faith in the same things. She also must have been extremely lovely to have been chosen by the King from among so many, but her security did not lie in her beauty, birth or position. She placed her trust firmly in the Lord and thus she became Queen and Vashti was deposed.

As the story unfolds we find Esther and all her people, the Jews, are under a death sentence. You'll need to read the whole story for yourself to grasp how serious things were. It really is exciting stuff. The only person who can save them is the King. Esther is urged by her uncle Mordecai to intercede with the King on behalf of her people. But, to as much as enter the King's presence without an invitation could mean death. Here is not another Vashti, confident in beauty and position. Esther is afraid. In spite of her fear, she fasts for three days, then throws herself on God as she goes in before the King. He is pleased and accepts her. When finally she uncovers the wickedness of her enemy Hamaan, the King puts him to death. What a remarkable woman Esther was. In humility and with prayer she broke the rules and traditions of her day, but she saved a nation. The King gave the evil Hamaan's estate, together with the seals of the kingdom, to her so that she might send out her own decrees to set her people free. Her eventual reward was to be trusted to rule and reign alongside the King.

Not all woman are destined to be prominent in the church, but then neither are all men. In the end it all comes back to the gifts which God has placed within each one of us and to the extent of our faith, which is also a gift of God. As you have by now gathered, I am convinced that there are enough examples of women in places of prominence, even in Old Testament days, for us to re-examine our own thoughts, feelings, hang-ups, prejudices and religious conditioning concerning their place today. I'm not demanding the right to be a man, I am simply asking for your active encouragement to be the woman God designed me to be. I only ask for your help to do the job for which he has equipped me without fear and hindrance from any of my brothers or sisters. What I ask for myself, I pray will also be available to every other child of God.

12

Some Thoughts from the New Testament

There is a long silence, biblically speaking, between
Malachi (the end of the Old Testament) and Matthew
(the beginning of the New) of about 400 years. The
silence was broken when the Holy Spirit visited Mary, a
young virgin girl. She accepted from God without question that she would become the mother of the promised
Messiah. Coming from her background and culture her
ready response was remarkable. The Eden promise
made to Eve was about to be fulfilled. Jesus was to be
born at a point in history which, for women, was an all
time low.

God did not choose Mary because she was down-
trodden, beaten and acquiescent. He chose her because
she knew him and was willing to lay the whole of her life
open to him. Mary was a girl of her time and she
understood what she was taking on. She knew that the
circumstances surrounding her first son's birth would
cause her pain, and that tongues would wag all through
her life. Even Joseph, the man she was to marry,
believed the worst until an angel had spoken to him
personally in a dream. It was only after this visitation
that he was able to go through with their marriage.

Mary counted the cost and fully realised what God was asking of her, but it would be worth all the hardship. The revelation dawned, 'From now on all generations shall call me blessed.' Perhaps today evangelical Christians should join in a little more freely and more often with the mighty throng throughout history who have blessed Mary for her obedience and sacrifice.

As Jesus grew into manhood, his understanding of himself and who he was grew. He knew that he was coming to fulfil one order and to establish a new one. He gathered his disciples around him, but no women were numbered among them. Some people see Jesus' choice as a statement which revealed the heavenly policy on women. It was the final nail in the coffin which was to bury all arguments for the case for female leadership. This fact should stop we ladies dead in our tracks! However, we're told that all Scripture must be looked at in context and, as I understand it, Jesus was sent first to 'the lost sheep of the house of Israel'. Before the gospel was to be made available to all men, God spoke first to his chosen people in the framework of their background and history. They rejected him. Jesus identified with the old order and then blew it apart. Nothing was left; no temple, no sacrifice, no law, no priesthood, but a new and higher order had been established. Now there was a living temple, Christ himself the only sacrifice. Love was the law, the church was the new nation of God and every believing man and woman was to be a priest.

If we are to be consistent in our reasoning, and we are saying that Jesus' selection of twelve men indicated his future attitude to women as leaders, we must also assume that it reflects his intentions for the Gentiles, as all of his apostles were Jews. His silence during his ministry on the subject of women in leadership is also taken as a reason for their disqualification. If only he had said one word in favour, but he didn't. But neither did he express his views on the future of circumcision which would have saved an awful lot of dissension in the early church and settled a debate which caused a great deal of pain and division back there. No, Jesus first fulfilled the law before doing away with it. He rendered the whole system redundant or 'obsolete' as Paul says. He ushered in a different kind of law altogether, as different as the butterfly is from the caterpiller. This law was not an external commandment leading to death, but an internal enabling giving life. It was not just for Jews but for all men and women of every race, tribe and tongue.

If you look closely you can see the signs of the new even before Jesus' death and resurrection. Ignorant women, who could neither read nor write, were being encouraged by Jesus to listen to his teaching and to learn from the Scriptures. That was revolutionary, as up to this point women had never been trusted in this way. Think about the bombshell Jesus dropped publicly in Luke 11:27−28. Here he is in a crowd and a woman cries out, 'Blessed is the mother who gave you birth and nursed you.' Speaking out of her culture and conditioning she desperately wanted to give recognition to a woman. The only way she felt she could do this was to refer to the part Mary played in his birth and upbringing. Jesus rebukes her in front of everyone, 'Blessed rather are those who hear the word of God and obey it.' Here was a new thought: women were not to be solely valued as son-bearers. They too could understand the word of God for themselves and obey it. This was the secret of Mary's commendation. It was her obedience, not only the child-bearing, that gained her the Father's approval. You can almost hear the silence, the indrawn breaths, as Jesus' hearers realised the significance of what he was saying.

Constantly during his ministry Jesus demonstrated his feeling towards women. I have already mentioned that a menstruating woman was not allowed to touch a man, let alone a teacher or a rabbi, and to do so meant death. In Matthew 9:20 Jesus found himself in just such a situation. Everything here was wrong. The woman had been bleeding for twelve long years. She should never have been out of her home, let alone in a crowd and touching a holy man. Jesus knew this, but he didn't need to rush off to cleanse himself ritually. He didn't raise a 'hue and cry'. He simply said, 'Take heart, daughter, your faith has healed you.' Today we find it hard to understand the implications of what was taking place when Jesus became involved in such incidents. It was not the miracle alone which was startling, but also the context.

Did you ever wonder why it was that the woman taken in adultery was brought to Jesus on her own? The very words 'being taken in adultery' imply that the couple were caught together in the act. Where was the man? The law demanded that both parties should be punished, but tradition had taken over and now the major responsibility for the sin rested with the woman. Women were sexual snares: men could not help themselves, they were caught in the temptress' web. Hereby hangs the argument for purdah. Women were the reason behind a man's downfall. Women led men into sexual sin, so cover them up and hide them away. Jesus threatened this thinking when in Matthew 5 he put the responsibility right back where it belonged. 'I tell you,' he said, 'that anyone who looks at a woman lustfully has already committed adultery with her in his heart.' From now on the men could no longer hide behind the traditions. They could no longer blame the women for their sinful actions, nor even for what went on in their hearts and minds.

Women were consistently singled out by Jesus for his special attention. The Samaritan woman was, I believe, the only person to whom Jesus personally revealed himself as the Messiah. This knowledge, according to John 4, turns her into the first rabid evangelist. Many Samaritans in the town where she lived believe in Jesus because of her testimony and enthusiasm for the good news. Women were at the cross when many of the men were missing. Mary, Jesus' mother, was also there— she who from the beginning knew something of his destiny. In John 19 we can read how, from the cross, Jesus gave his mother to his closest friend and disciple, John, and he also gave John to Mary. I don't believe that in doing this Jesus was simply providing for Mary's old age. More likely he knew that they would need one another in the on-going work of the church. Jesus revealed himself first to a woman after the resurrection. Mary Magdalene came to the tomb and found it empty. Instead of a corpse she found a risen Lord who sent her back to tell the other disciples that he was alive. It is quite amazing when you re-read the Gospels with the intent of discovering the place of women in Jesus' ministry. You find them involved over and over again at the very heart of all that he did and said. I've mentioned only a few of the numerous references to women in the Gospels, it is a worth-while exercise to read and study them in greater depth. Now I want to take a look at the epistles and the Acts of the Apostles.

In my own experience over the years, one teaching from the Scriptures which has been misunderstood, and therefore misused, is that of the submission of wives to husbands. It appears in 1 Peter 3, Colossians 3 and Ephesians 5, and on the face of it is quite clear and straightforward. However, we do need to understand that these instructions concern the social structure. They help us to survive in a world and society which is less than perfect and they give us a framework to enable us to live and work in harmony. These guidelines are given, not just to husbands and wives, but to children and parents and to slaves and masters, or, in modern terms, to employers and employees. Elsewhere we are told how to respond to national leaders and governments. But we have already seen that 'in Christ' these structures do not exist. There is no male or female, no bond or free and no Jew or Greek.

If we accept the restrictions of society and adopt a submissive attitude to its structures, insofar as our conscience before God allows, then in the church we can freely discover how the Spirit wants to use us and order our relationships. Thus the company director is not automatically made an elder in the church—it might well be a clerk from among his office staff. The school music teacher is not necessarily first choice to lead the worship—it could well be one of his pupils on whom the anointing rests. Of course, it would be unthinkable that a lazy clerk or a rebellious teenager should be given authority, any more than a mean director or an apathetic music teacher. Similarly, a wife who is submissive to her husband may well find herself, with his approval, taking up some form of leadership in the church to which he in turn is happy to be subject. All must be done decently and in order. In this way we are all subject to one another, just like the various instruments in an orchestra. Sometimes one plays and the others are silent; sometimes they all play together. They follow the conductor and the score; we follow the Spirit and the word.

The same applies to parents and children. It is totally acceptable for a young man to earn the right to become a leader of a church with his parents as part of the congregation. Why then are we so adamant about keeping wives immobilised as far as functioning in the

church is concerned when they have proved their loy-
alty and submissiveness at home? In 1 Corinthians 2:3–
11 it talks about the head of the man being Christ, and
the head of the woman being man. Here the word
'head' would be better rendered 'source'. Christ is the
'source' of life and release to the husband, the husband
is the 'source' of life and release to the wife. Please note
that not all men are the 'source' of all women, the
husband is the 'source' of the wife! 'Source' is more to
do with supply and freedom than rule and restriction. If
Christ supplies and releases husbands, then they should
do the same for their wives, which is exactly the argument Paul puts forward in Ephesians 5:25–33. An
unsubmissive wife in the social order will prevent her
husband from taking up his office in the church. An
unloving husband can equally prevent his wife from
taking up her role on the same basis. This, I believe, is
God's order.

Once her ministry is accepted in the church, a
woman doesn't have to clear her contributions through
her husband, but through the leadership of the church.
Obviously, if he is part of that team she submits her
contribution to him on that basis, not because of their
marriage. In today's church, as a testimony and example to the world, there must be no discrimination on the
basis of sex, colour or class. I may still, however, in the
natural order of things, happen to be female, British
and middle-class, but for me as a child of God the
kingdom has also come. Now I live in two worlds and
need to show clearly how I can live God's order in both
at the same time without conflict.

These two chapters on the Bible are not designed to
be an exhaustive study of the Scriptures. I simply want
to share some thoughts which have helped me over the
years. They have enabled me to ask some questions and
rock the boat a little, and maybe find a few answers into

the bargain. So, let me continue with my ramble through the New Testament.

Next, I'd like to draw your attention to a husband and wife team, Aquila and Priscilla. They are very interesting. You'll find them mentioned in Acts 18:1, 1 Corinthians 16 and Romans 16. They travelled with Paul. Well, I suppose that could be explained away by saying that Priscilla went along to wash the socks had there not been so much recorded about them both. To start with they had a church in their home. They were also Paul's 'helpers in Christ' his 'fellow workers' who 'risked their necks' for him and 'all the Gentile churches thanked them'. Together they were deeply involved with Paul in ministry—not quite so easy to explain away! Finally, together they taught Apollos 'more accurately the way of God', and there are scriptures which seem to indicate Apollos was an apostle. Certainly in 1 Corinthians 1 and 3 he is put alongside Peter and Paul. So, this husband and wife were quite a team, and Priscilla was quite a lady to be teaching a man of such standing in the early church.

Obviously, some would say, her husband really took pride of place. She was possibly a helper, but never in the driver's seat. Theologians themselves knock that idea on the head. They tell us that where two names are used together, like Priscilla and Aquila, the first name shows predominance. In other words, it indicates who took the lead in the situation. In the case of Barnabas and Paul, Barnabas took the lead to begin with. Later the roles were reversed when Paul became predominant. Apparently, Luke who wrote the Acts was not just trying to be polite by occasionally putting Priscilla first!

The New Testament is littered with references to women doing all kinds of work. In Romans 16 we have Phoebe a deaconess. The word is translated elsewhere as 'servant', and at times 'minister'. Paul encourages the saints to 'help her in anything she might need'. He personally gives her authority and underlines the fact that she has helped many others apart from himself. Here is a woman in a travelling ministry, sent with Paul's blessing and authority. In the same passage there is talk about Mary 'who worked hard among you'. Doing what, I wonder? Making the tea and sandwiches or ironing the creases out of the scrolls? And how about Junia (Romans 16:7)? She was a Christian before Paul. She had been in prison with him and was 'of note among the apostles'. Watchman Nee, in his book *The Normal Christian Church Life* is clearly convinced that she was counted, not only among the apostles, but as a noted apostle herself.

Finally, there are the 'older women' mentioned in the letter to Titus. I don't for one moment think that 'older' means aged because they would never have coped with all that was asked of them. It simply means mature in their understanding of God and without heavy family responsibilities. These women were encouraged to 'teach what is good' and also to 'train younger women'. It is stretching the imagination too far to believe that 'teaching what is good' meant that they were confined to cookery and needlework! Oh, and there are lots more women in the New Testament if you care to do a little research. This is a very worth-while study and will help you to see the wealth of evidence there is in the Scripture to show how women were involved and used in the early church. There is much more support for their ministry than for some other major doctrines we hold dear. We would indeed be shocked to feel that they were challenged on the basis of infrequent mentions.

In concluding this chapter on the New Testament, I'd like to do what some would consider to be typically feminine and irrational. I'd like to close with a verse from the Psalms. I'm quoting from the Amplified Bible, Psalm 68:11, 'The Lord gives the word [of power]; the women who bear and publish (the news) are a great host.'

13

The Difficult Scriptures

Now I'd like to take a look at what are often called the 'problem' or 'difficult' scriptures. That there are problems is without question true. In a series of articles by David Pawson in *Renewal* magazine, the writer states: 'We turn then to what are frequently called the "problem" passages in the Pauline corpus. However, they present "problems" only to those who have a very different understanding of the total Biblical context to the exposition already outlined in these articles.' Within three paragraphs he goes on to say: '...when taking part in public worship through prayer or prophecy, whether this involved a veil (not a hat!) or longer hair than men, is not altogether clear.' [1] So even for someone who is quite sure that there are no problems if you take the scriptures at face value and in their plainest meaning, there are still a few problems!

Of course, the Christians to whom Paul was writing had the advantage of the original letter written in a

---

[1] Pawson, David, 'Leadership Is Male', *Renewal*. (March 1988), p. 28.

language that was familiar to them. Furthermore, they did not have to cope with numerous uninspired translations, compiled almost exclusively by men who, although sincere, were in most cases conditioned by male-dominated backgrounds and had their minds fairly made up before they ever came to the writing desk. Today, we have the complete New Testament Scriptures to help us get things into context and perspective. However, this doesn't always simplify things in the way that David Pawson implies. It means that every theologian and professor of the Scriptures worth his salt, few whose integrity we doubt, claims with David that his particular view is backed up by the rest of the Holy Book. Ordinary saints like me, who don't understand the nuances of the Greek, are still having to make up their own minds prayerfully before God as to what they believe.

In fact, within Team Spirit, the ministry team of which I am a member, we have often debated these issues. We found there were two opinions. While everyone agreed that women should be encouraged to utilise all their gifts, some still maintained that they should not have governmental authority. This was by no means a disaster, as we see our relationships of primary importance and continue to work together, respecting one another's differing views.

In her book, *Woman in the Bible*, Mary Evans takes twelve pages to expound 1 Corinthians 11:1–16. She calls upon the opinions of no less than fifteen theologians in this context alone. These men had an amazing variety of thought, research and explanation to offer us. This kind of work is really helpful and important. It sheds so much light on the ambiguous translation of words and phrases, as well as the customs of the day. Nevertheless, when such learned and eminent men disagree, we are left with the responsibility of hearing what the Spirit is saying to us as individuals.

When the charismatic renewal hit the church about twenty-five years ago many controversies raged. Is love more important than the gifts? Do you have to speak in tongues? Are 'tongues' an evidence of the Holy Spirit's indwelling? without the sign of 'tongues' are you really filled with the Spirit? Could the experience be termed a second blessing? Does the Bible actually say much at all about the fullness of the Spirit? The arguments and discussions were as hotly contested then as the issue of women in leadership is today. The debate on the baptism of the Holy Spirit is still going on after a quarter of a century in some churches. The practices, however, are increasingly accepted as more and more people are coming into the experience. They see the Scriptures in a fresh light and where there once appeared little support for their new-found blessing, now every page seems to carry the message. This is also true for many who are searching for a new appreciation for the role of women.

A friend of mine, who comes from a stream which has not been entirely at rest about the charismatic issue, was filled with the Holy Spirit while preaching— a little embarrassing to say the least! His testimony is that it took two years for his theology to catch up with his experience. So it is for many Christians as they wrestle with the difficulties of accepting women in leadership. Dave Tomlinson, another close friend, struggled with the historical conditioning his Brethren background had left him with. He became aware of an inward change of heart, but still had to face the years of ingrained teaching and a particular approach to the Bible. He spent four years talking, thinking, praying and studying until he is now totally convinced from all angles, of the place for women in the leadership structures of the church at all levels.

So what am I trying to say in all of this? My own conviction is that the Holy Spirit is speaking to us afresh on this subject and we must try to look behind the interpretation of Scripture which we have inherited. Should you find within you the feeling that to do this would be a betrayal of those who have taught you, or a sense that what was good enough for them is good enough for you, I would strongly suggest that you stop and ask the Holy Spirit if these thoughts come from him or not.

After having read the various arguments about the passage from 1 Corinthians 11, what do I gain from it when I read it for myself? What jumps out of the verses at me are two circles. Two heavy gold rings with carving on them. Hold on for a minute; don't skip over this paragraph! I did warn you right at the beginning that we were going to look at things with the imagination, and this is one of those times. Here are my two wedding rings, for in my mind that's what they are. The first ring is contained in verse 3. The carving is: Lord-man-woman-man-God and so back round the circle again.

The source of all life and the source of all things is God. Without doubt nothing that lives comes into being without the Father. Likewise everything returns to him. This interpretation seems far more in keeping with the rest of Scripture. For example, Ezekiel in his vision of the heavenly structure saw that it was wheels within wheels, not a series of ladders. Why must we insist on breaking these two circles and making them into ladders? God's heart is not for a hierarchy, but a fellowship. His authority is not the goal, but a means to an end. The end is friendship and becoming joint heirs with Christ Jesus. In the kingdom there are no ladders of authority and chains of command even though that may have been our experience in the church. We live in a world that teaches aggressively, 'If you don't tread on his head, he'll tread on yours.' We see life as an upward progression, to be gained by passing others along the way and keeping some in their place.

This attitude has also found its way into our church structure and fellowship life. God's view is interdependency; man and woman made in his image. We cannot divide the Godhead up and give one person the top slot. Father, Son and Spirit are together God. Separately each is in harmony with the others. So it is with the creation made in the image of God; husband and wife in maturity together reflecting the image of God. Separately they are equally important; each is made to be in harmony with the others. Just as you cannot divide the Godhead, you cannot divide the creation. We are interdependent and we need one another.

I don't want to ignore the other sections of this same scripture, but I must be honest and say that if I have to take them at face value, without thought or question, then I am lost! We seem to get ourselves so bogged down in hats and veils, long and short hair. Is the apostle not trying to speak to us about attitudes, albeit through the culture of that time and place? Wouldn't it be a little eccentric if a twentieth-century woman, like myself, were to wear first-century clothing? We would certainly get a few strange looks. Isn't he asking us not to prove that we are free by purposefully flaunting the cultural conventions of our day? As a liberated Christian woman I shouldn't feel the need deliberately to shock my contemporaries to underline my point. When I was a girl, many ladies of easy virtue wore a chain around their ankles. If I had attempted to do the same, my mother would have skinned me alive! Today, lots of girls and women wear ankle chains, and it certainly doesn't mean what it did when I was young. There is nothing to be gained by keeping our daughters from wearing them. Head coverings, be they hats or veils, surely come into this category.

A Jewish woman, to show her changed status from virgin to married woman, tied up her hair and covered her head. The tradition of the day was that the greater a woman's piety, the less you saw of her head. In fact it led to the practice of some orthodox women shaving their heads and wearing a wig. In this way their heads were always covered. This kind of legalism led to some women even wearing something on their heads in bed, which sounds a little way-out. One would assume that only her husband was in the bed with her, or perhaps it was because of the angels! Today, many women have the same hairstyle for years, both when single and married. Gone is the Victorian and Edwardian custom of putting up your hair when you reached a certain age. So, for us, the question of hairstyles is irrelevant.

Perhaps if I wanted to prove my liberty in my culture, I might refuse to take my husband's name, or to wear a wedding ring—all in the name of freedom. If the angels do actually need some sign of authority from me, I can't think that a huge hat adorned with flowers or fruit, or a carefully crocheted doily, or indeed a 'Marks & Sparks' scarf would do it for them, or even, for that matter, an original Corinthian veil covering all of me. I'm sure that the angels are too intelligent to be fooled in that way. They, like the Lord himself, are looking for signs in my lifestyle and attitudes which prove that my heart is after God. After all, even under the Old Covenant David broke the law by eating the shewbread which only the priests were allowed to touch. Nevertheless, he was also commended, not for keeping every jot and tittle of the law, but because his heart was after God. That's the kind of commendation I should like to receive from Father.

And what about hair? How on earth does nature

teach us that it is shameful for a man to have long hair?
There must be some explanation which we don't understand. If a man were not to cut his hair it would simply
go on growing, as would his beard. If a sign of modesty
and submission in a woman is long hair, how does my
African sister get on when her hair doesn't grow very
long anyway? And who determines how long 'long' is?
Hairdressers will tell you that each person's hair grows
to its own optimum length. Some hair starts breaking at
a certain point. My hairdresser cuts off broken ends to
encourage growth, but he tells me that for some people,
at a certain length, it keeps breaking and broken hair
just doesn't grow. We do seem to be on very shaky
ground when arguing the case for a literal acceptance of
this passage, with no room for interpretation at all. The
state of our hair is not a relevant issue today, unless in
some way, by length or style, we identify with, say, a
cult or sect. Neither, in my opinion, is whether your
hair is straight or curly, red or brown, or purple or
green. Our heart attitude really is what God is looking
for. Naturally, if some section of the community, which
in some way was diametrically opposed to Jesus,
started to wear straight hair with a silver bow as a sign
of their unbelief, I would avoid that fashion like the
plague and advise other Christians to do the same.
Apart from that I want to love, in a right relationship
with the Lord, my husband and all my brothers and
sisters, hair or no hair, hat or no hat.

Now to 1 Corinthians 14:33–34. Here again if I am
asked to take the words as they come, and am expected
to believe that I should never speak in a church meeting, it really doesn't make sense at all. In verse 34 it
apparently cites the law to back up this demand for
silence, but the law does not support this. Nowhere are
women commanded to keep quiet. In fact the very
opposite is indicated by Eli's remarks to Hannah. He

thought she was drunk because she was praying silently! One minute we are told to be silent, the next we are encouraged to pray and prophesy. So the Scripture appears to contradict itself! Granted, you could do the former silently, but certainly not the latter. I suppose an alternative would be to write everything down and pass it to one of the men, but that would not have been possible as many of the women were illiterate, and anyway they didn't have biros and post-it pads then....

Seriously, it is all to do with orderliness during the meetings. If everyone had the right to interrupt or to ask questions at any time, it scarcely would have been done 'in a fitting and orderly way', as required in verse 40. Women were particularly called to keep their questions to themselves and ask their husband at a more appropriate time. The reason for this almost certainly had to do with the fact that men were more educated in these matters than the women. These particular women, if they were Jewish believers, might at *best* know the traditions, but would never have been taught the law. If they were non-Jewish, they would know neither the traditions nor the law. Half a dozen women like myself in the meeting, all asking 'why?', would have caused bedlam. Especially as in some cases they sat on one side of the meeting room while the men sat on the other. In Christ women were coming into a new phase and freedom. They needed some guidelines to help them adjust.

While on the subject of women keeping silent, I should like to share an experience I had in counselling. There was a group of women, six or seven as I remember it, who all wanted to be baptised in the Holy Spirit. I wasn't involved from the beginning, but at a later stage. Some folks had laid hands on them and prayed for them. The results were a little disconcerting and all the ladies were affected in the same way. They were in floods of tears and felt very uncomfortable. They wanted to run from the room and some confessed to an overwhelming desire to scream aloud. None of them had felt that they were filled with the Spirit; none had experienced speaking in tongues, nor any other gift for that matter. I listened to one after the other explaining their plight. They were all married except one and she was the daughter of one of the women present. Their husbands, and the girl's father, had all received the Holy Spirit and spoken in tongues, but not these ladies.

I discovered an evil spirit at work among them. It was a religious spirit directly connected with their background. I bound its activity, cast it out and all the women were immediately released from its influence. Finally, amid new tongues, tears of joy and laughter, and encouragement from their men, we discovered that they came from a background which had in the past demanded that women be silent. How Satan had enjoyed binding and immobilising these daughters of the King. We need to be sure when dealing with one another that we don't get too academic and lose sight of our God-given directives. Like Paul, we also have a commission to set the prisoners free. We must never be a party to any form of enslavement to the Enemy of our souls.

The other scripture that I want to look at here is 1 Timothy 2:8–15. Once again, if we take the superficial meaning of the words, there is quite a lot of explaining to do. I like the injunction that all men, when praying, should hold their holy hands up in the air. It certainly might stop those long boring prayers which some men pray, because their arms would go numb. Then the women are encouraged to dress modestly and only wear cheap clothes, never any jewellery. Are we to assume from these verses that women are not allowed to hold up holy hands, and that men are permitted to dress extravagantly? No, of course not. Paul is addressing particular situations in the groups or churches which Timothy was responsible for, and we need to keep this in mind. He is not making one indelible rule for women and another for men. This is reinforced when we realise that these two men had been working together by now for a number of years. In view of this, is it not likely that if these instructions concerning women were universally taught by Paul, Timothy would have already been very familiar with them?

'A woman should learn in quietness and full submission,' Paul continues. In our society this would sound like an indictment against women. We must, however, put these words into context. 'A woman should learn,' was almost the equivalent of causing an atomic explosion in a culture where the women were kept in darkness and forbidden any kind of education. No wonder he added 'in...full submission'! I can just see these women suddenly given their freedom and taking full advantage of the situation to make their presence felt in every way possible. We already know that the prevailing attitude among rabbis was to ignore women as spiritual beings. Another Jewish gent called Eleazer said, 'Let the words of the law be burned rather than committed to women.' They felt quite strongly about it, didn't they? We have a Christian equivalent around today, as some men feel that a woman is incapable of holding on to spiritual truth, believe it or not. Here is Paul, a rabbi, instructing Timothy to teach the women. The whole congregation must have erupted on hearing this. Women were no longer to be simply air brains and sex symbols; no longer were they to be segregated and ignored; they were to be taught! No longer would their time in church be spent in gossiping about who was marrying whom and how many babies everyone had; they were to learn!

The Jewish women knew, like parrots, the traditions. It was the women who kept their homes kosher. They washed the baby's hands the ritual number of times to make them clean and did a thousand other tasks, but they had never been taught the Scriptures. Keeping silent and not being allowed to teach needs to be seen in the light of their present ignorance, not as a restriction for all time. Learning must come to an end and the process of giving out must begin at some time. We can see that this was advised for the more mature ladies in Titus 2:3. In 1 Timothy 1:3–7 the young leader has not to allow certain men to teach false doctrines. Surely this request was much the same thing? None of us wants to listen to harmful rubbish from anyone, whether man or woman. If, however, a woman applies herself and studies her subject achieving excellence, do we steadfastly say we will not be taught by her solely because she is a woman?

The next verse in our passage is also very interesting and needs careful examination: 'I do not permit a woman to teach or to have authority over a man; she must be silent.' The Authorised Version, which so many of the old school love, puts it: '...to usurp authority and teach.' The word 'usurp' is used only once in Scripture and carries with it connotations of sex and violence. It is a very strong word. It would appear that these newly liberated women were taking full advantage of their Christian 'rights' and using their freedom to degrade their husbands, in public, with innuendo. It could be said, without destroying the meaning of the text, that Paul was not forbidding them to teach, rather he was denying them the right to put down the existing authority or leadership when teaching. I've heard plenty of men do just that, and I'm sure Paul would have restricted anyone who was praying, preaching or prophesying in conflict with appointed leaders.

Teaching itself is, of course, another whole subject. If we are going to forbid women to do it, we must clearly define what we mean by the word. Teaching can take place in a variety of ways. Eve certainly didn't persuade Adam to eat the forbidden fruit by preaching a three point message on the virtues of the tree of knowledge. And if we women are instructed to prophesy, which incidentally is also a very difficult word to define, does this not contain aspects of teaching? I am convinced that it's not teaching that Paul was worried about, but the usurping of authority. Women who, like Eve, make strong assertions when not in command of all the facts are dangerous. Even more so when they poke fun at, and 'murder', their husbands or leaders in public.

While on this same verse, it may be worth pointing out that in 1 Corinthians 7:10–12, Paul goes to great length to explain the difference between what is his personal request, and what is a command from the Lord. There are plenty of students of the word who feel that when Paul says 'I', that is exactly what he means, and it could not be considered as an unchangeable and irrefutable word from God, or even something that every other apostle practised. Under these conditions, where the women are only just beginning to learn, or where they are using their freedom wrongly, anyone would be foolish to permit them to teach. It would, without question, be an unqualified disaster.

'For Adam was formed first, then Eve. And Adam was not the one deceived; it was the woman who was deceived and became a sinner. But women will be saved through childbirth, if they continue in faith, love and holiness with propriety.' Phew! There's quite a bit in these verses which leaves us wondering exactly what Paul meant. If you want an excellent paper which covers these and other scriptures, you might like to read

Roger Forster's *New Humanity*.[1] There are some inconsistencies here if the words of these verses need no
explanation. We saw that in all seriousness we cannot
have all men putting their hands up immediately they
pray. It's an encouragement, not a command. By the
same argument, neither can we insist that all women
must have children in order to be saved. Some married
women are unable to become pregnant for medical
reasons, whereas other women have chosen to remain
single. There must be some other way of looking at
Paul's comment. Verse 15 actually reads: 'But woman
[singular] will be saved...if they [plural] continue in
faith.' Here Paul is referring to the promise to Eve of a
seed that would bruise Satan's head. That seed came
through Mary and was Jesus. Eve, 'the mother of all
living', shares in the salvation which that particular
birth brings, as do all women who continue in faith. It's
faith that saves women, not having children!

Back to verse 13 and the statement that Adam was
formed first. Only people who insist on their ladders
rather than my circles think this must mean superiority.
If 'first' means a kind of higher order, then Adam must
be subject to the animals. Quite the contrary. Adam
being the last of God's creation was the triumphant
culmination. I'm not saying in this that Eve was to have
supremacy, but simply that it was not good for God's
pièce de résistance to be alone. It was not good in the
garden, it was not good in the New Testament church,
and it is not good today. The instruction, 'A woman
should learn,' must be kept in view while studying this
whole section. Eve was created to be with Adam. She
was deceived, very possibly, because Adam didn't do a
good job of teaching and explaining to her the ground

---

[1] Roger Forster, *New Humanity*, Ichthus Fellowship, 116 Perry
    Vale, London SE23 2LQ.

rules. Some would try to tell us that Adam was not deceived and this makes Eve the greater sinner. How can that be? As we saw earlier, surely Adam knew exactly what he was doing and was therefore primarily responsible? That's why Paul in Romans 5 points out that sin entered in by one 'man'. So, 'a woman should learn'. Don't isolate women and keep them in ignorance. That's how they were deceived in the first place.

I tackled the question of whether women are more likely to be deceived in chapter 3, so I'll not go over that ground again. However, I would like to point out that in other parts of Scripture we are warned 'to allow no one to deceive us' where the word for 'no one' covers both men and women. Here are a few references for you: 'Let no-one deceive you with empty words' (Eph 5:6). 'Do not deceive yourselves' (1 Cor 3:18). 'Don't let anyone deceive you in any way' (2 Thess 2:3). 'Watch out that no-one deceives you' (Mt 24:4). 'Do not let anyone lead you astray' (1 Jn 3:7). There are many more. I find it incredible, if Paul is trying to make a point about woman's susceptibility to deception, that this is not backed up by other scriptures. The rest of the Bible makes it clear that all—men and women—are vulnerable. Surely women need to learn in order to stand equipped, alongside the men, making a stronger team as God originally designed in the garden.

I don't suppose for one moment that I've answered all your questions about these scriptures. I don't honestly think I could, even given more time and space. I do hope, however, I've helped you to look at them from another angle. At least maybe you'll understand that those of us who see things differently are not wanting to sweep what the Bible teaches under the carpet. I see the word of God as being incredibly important and do not desire to do anything, knowingly, which conflicts with, or contradicts, the Father heart of God.

14

God's Rubik Cube

Where do we go from here? Many people must be asking this question as they come into a new understanding of the potential for women in God's work. There are two things which I'm praying will not happen. The first is that we do nothing. The second is that we try to put the clock back. If we do nothing confusion will remain and increase, and Satan will be delighted. Women will continue to be restricted, as will the forward move of the church and the spread of the gospel. The various streams of church life will harden in their attitudes and retreat into their emphases, with each one doing their own thing. If we put the clock back, we will be in danger of becoming even more irrelevant to the world than we are now. Men and women in society, as well as the church, are searching for a practical reality that works. They will no longer be placated with 'pie in the sky when we die'. We must think and pray things through, examine the evidence and debate. But whatever we do, we must not stand still or go backwards. Let's take a fresh and careful look at the Bible and also church history. Both have much to teach us.

You see, this is not a new dilemma. In the sixth

century, a council of churches met together in France to
debate: 'Do women have souls?' The final count was in
favour of the motion by one vote. Since those days we
have made some progress, but still the Enemy contends
every step of the way in spite of some very enlightened
periods in history. As you study and pray, please ask
the Holy Spirit to light things up for you, so that you
have your own personal revelation. Keep your hearts
free from wrong attitudes and repent of past conditioning wherever you see it. Ask the Lord to deal with
jealousy, bitterness, fear, feminism and chauvinism.
Not only do these things harm us spiritually and naturally, they also act like coloured spectacles, distorting
our view of the world and everything that happens in it.
Our bad responses and conditioning add colour to our
spectacles, the strength of which varies according to the
depth of our experience. For example, in a totally different area, some of the older generation who have
survived the world wars, have a warped view of the
German nation which, to say the least, needs adjusting.
Such phrases as, 'The only good German is a dead one,'
have passed on prejudice and affected generations of
Europeans to this day. Again, in the deep south of
North America, I heard this comment made about a
white man's untidy yard (or garden as we would call
it): 'Looks like a bunch of niggers live there.'

Some influences go very deep and the spectacles we
wear are dark and almost blinding. Do ask the Lord to
reveal to you your specific areas of damage where the
Enemy has affected you, and claim them back from
Satan. To say you have none is to be deceived. If you
were that perfect you'd already have your resurrection
body. Let's discover these 'toe holds' the Enemy has
and make sure we eradicate them from our lives.

We must encourage one another, particularly when
we see God's gifts in operation, even when it doesn't fit

our idea of how male or female should function. Let us be sympathetic and long-suffering with one another as we move towards maturity. Most people have insecurities and problems. Communication is often difficult with those we love and trust, and at times it is impossible when we are faced with people who disagree with our particular viewpoint. Winning arguments and swapping scriptures is not the answer. Staying in our own small corner with its fortifications against invasion and change is not the answer either. Viewing ourselves as being part of the same family, admitting how we feel and opening ourselves up and listening to different perspectives without losing our integrity is the answer. We should find this a challenging and enlarging experience, not a destroying one.

There is a saying that 'the exception proves the rule'. Christians quote this same saying when addressing the notable women leaders of the Bible. My advice is, if your theology only allows you occasional exceptions, then at least be active in looking for them and wherever you find one encourage her with all your heart. In saying that God may allow one now and again, the door is open to others. So if you live under an authority in your church that only has room for exceptions make sure that you are one of them. We may all get in on that ticket. In fact, I believe we may well become buried under a heap of exceptions during the next decade.

Exceptions certainly need plenty of love and understanding. The fact that they are unusual makes them feel strange and out of place, without them being told so. Let us back up those of exceptional gifts who have been given to us by our God. Don't let's see them as oddities, wondering at them and viewing them with distaste and distrust. Rather, let us encourage them and ensure that they accomplish everything the Lord

designed them for. Let me remind you of some of the
church's recent exceptions.

I mentioned Gladys Aylward and Jackie Pullinger in
an earlier chapter. Both are remarkable ladies and both
worked among needy Chinese people. You can follow
Jackie's story by getting hold of her book *Chasing the
Dragon*. This recounts her experiences working with
drug addicts within the Walled City of Hong Kong.
Gladys defied the mission selection boards and followed
the Spirit into an amazing series of adventures with
orphan children in mainland China. The lives of these
women are a wonderful testimony and example for us
and should inspire many others to seek the Lord for
their own release into his service. Today Jackie is in the
process of building a church from the dregs of society
now changed into God's trophies of grace.

I could hardly complete a book like this without
referring to one or two other women who have exceptional gifts and callings. General Eva Burrows of the
Salvation Army is a single lady who leads an organisation which numbers two million worldwide. Jean Dar-
nall is also a lady of worldwide renown. She has just
celebrated fifty years in a preaching and healing ministry. It all began for her as a teenager when the Lord
healed her from a progressive kidney disease. As a
result of her healing, most of her family were saved and
she embarked on her remarkable calling. Jill Dann, an
Anglican, is perhaps not a household name, but she has
served on the General Synod of the Church of England
for years. Among other things she filled the chair of the
Evangelical Council vacated by John Stott, and is at
present Vice-Chairman of the House of Laity of the
General Synod—a very prestigious position! These are
but a few of many women through whom God is working today. I trust in the closing decade of this millen-
nium there will be an ever-increasing number.

As I draw my book to a close I think it would be appropriate to focus on history's greatest exception. Not a woman, but a man—Jesus himself. He stands unique among us all, indeed among the whole creation. To say there's no one like Jesus is the understatement of all time. He put the full stop to one sentence of history and started an entirely new one. He closed the door on sin and death and opened the gate into holiness and life. As the last Adam he put paid to a helpless and doomed race and became the first of a new generation—the ongoing generation of Jesus Christ.

There are those who use Jesus' maleness as an argument against my sex. They insist that because he was a man, masculinity alone truly reflects the fullness of the Godhead, but they have missed the point completely. When creating Adam the Lord put his image into the man, but because it was not good for him to be alone, God divided up Adam. From this point God's attributes would be seen in the man and woman together. The great picture of the glorified Christ in Revelation 1 reveals Jesus as 'a son of man...with a golden girdle round his [female] breasts'. This gives us a New Testament understanding of the old name for God, 'El Shaddai', which has within its meaning 'female breasts'. In this vision of the glorified Christ, and in the picture of the church as a many-membered person with Jesus as the head, all the masculine and feminine distinctives are once again in place. Only as we are united in Christ together can we fully represent God, who is 'in all' and who 'will be what he will be'.

During Jesus' suffering and death on the cross his side was opened up by the spear of a Roman soldier and out flowed the water and the blood, his 'double cure' for the guilt and power of sin. From this flow out of Christ into the world, a bride suitable for him was formed and the church came into being. But this outpouring in no way depleted him. Rather than allowing something to drain out of himself into the church, leaving him incomplete (as was the case with Adam), Jesus opened up a river of life which was, is now, and ever shall be, available to us all.

The river will never diminish with the drinking. The more it flows the more there is to come. It is the river of his grace and it issues directly from his throne. Christ and his bride are now one. She is his body, he is her source. She has nothing which did not come from him and she is the full expression of all that he is. All the masculinity and femininity of God are there in perfect harmony in Christ and his bride. They are completely one with another and with the Father and with the Holy Spirit.

Sex, not to be confused with masculinity or femininity, was a necessary factor in the process of bringing forth the people of God on the earth, but it becomes superfluous when the earthly people have been transformed into the heavenly. Sexual activity, wonderful and God-given though it is, disappears, giving way and being fulfilled in Christ's relationship to his bride. Masculinity and femininity remain, expressed now, not only in God, but also in the diversity of his people.

Of course Jesus was a man in human terms and I've absolutely no desire to produce a Lord with a mixed-up gender, a kind of physical hotch-potch. However, I don't believe that in admitting this obvious fact it somehow mitigates against my sex in any way. There is a mystery here. Jesus was in every way a man, but he was also God. He was tempted and he overcame in all points, not for just one sex but for all mankind. The pain he suffered far outweighed the pain of childbirth or any torture that man could inflict. The love he showed us far outshines the love of a man for a woman, or a mother for her child. The satanic assault upon his mind went far beyond the understanding of psychiatry, or the madness experienced by men. He overcame in every area of human weakness for all mankind, passing completely beyond our understanding, so that now he is the answer for all our ills. He descended into hell and emerged triumphant! Don't let us, for a single second, reduce Jesus and what he accomplished to mere human understanding. He was not even dependent on a man for his birth, life or resurrection. What he did was infinite and eternal. Thank you, Jesus.

If we continue to misunderstand God's intention with gender; should a man hold to male authority or even superiority, with leadership in the church being exclusively male, this very attitude itself will foster within him feelings of thankfulness for his manliness in a rather specific way. Even though this is unconscious it will almost certainly be there. Like the Jews I mentioned earlier, our Christian men will end up thanking God for making them male, and believing, even if it is unspoken, that to be female is undesirable. Under these circumstances, for a man to discover even a trace of femininity in himself would be completely unacceptable. However, no one living is either totally masculine or completely feminine; each has an element of the other in a variety of strengths of expression. Pride and fear will be the outcome of such views, and these will be more than enough to maintain the barriers between the sexes. God did not build a clear wall of partition. We can see this in the way the church is described in Scripture. The role of the church in the world is to be the body of Christ. We are his body, so in that sense, we are clearly masculine. The role of the church to Christ himself is that of a bride. Here we become totally feminine. The virgin bride coming to maturity and readiness is waiting for Christ, the bridegroom, to return so that together they can enjoy the greatest wedding feast of all time. In relation to the Enemy, the church becomes an army. Armies historically are heavily weighted on the masculine side, but not exclusively so. We have seen with Deborah and Jael that there is a place for women in warfare. The army then contains both elements. Finally, we see the church's role to the Father and to the Holy Spirit as that of a temple, a dwelling place for God which is neutral.

So, then, if we lay aside the purely sexual aspects, we discover that there are masculine and feminine traits in God the Father, in Christ, in the church and also in every individual believer. And of course there is the Holy Spirit who is clearly referred to as 'he', nevertheless the Hebrew word for 'Spirit' is feminine, as is the Greek word for 'dove'.

Recognising that we must observe the social structures, and that the Lord calls us to be submissive in our attitudes to him and to one another, why should we put a ceiling on anyone for the way in which God may want to use them? All through church history, during times of revival and the Spirit's moving, women have been used by God. Not least, they have been counted worthy to shed their blood for their belief in the gospel. The Montanists in the second century had well-known prophetesses. Waldensians in the twelfth century were considered shocking, all because they had women preachers. Many Anabaptists who died in the sixteenth century for their teaching were women. The Moravians in the eighteenth century had female elders, and the Quakers never made any distinction between male and female believers. Wesley was also an ardent believer in the place of women, despite his bad experiences in his own marriage. William Booth of the Salvation Army in the last century said, 'Some of my best men are women.' The statement may be a rather backhanded compliment, and by today's standards would be considered to be a sexist remark, but he highly valued women in his work. Luther took pains to underline from 1 Peter 2:9 that the royal priesthood embraced every member of the church: man, woman and child. The office of presbyteress, which had been a leading function in the early church, was actually only disallowed at the Council of Laodicea in AD 363.

God, and God alone, has fitted and equipped us for the task which he has in mind. Let us not be guilty of telling him what he can or cannot do with his creation. Fulfilment can only be found by accepting and fitting into the place Father has lovingly planned and designed for us, and there is room for us all. It says in 1 Corinthians 13:12, 'Now we see but a poor reflection; then we shall see face to face.' If we really believe this statement to be true, let's admit that we are still learners. Let's agree that there is more revelation on the subject of how we relate as men and women for us to see, and let us remain open to the Lord, to his word and to one another.

A few years ago, you could hardly enter a home without seeing that colourful Rubik Cube puzzle. Everyone, it seemed, was bent on trying to achieve what was, mathematically, almost impossible without some guidelines or instructions. The combination of options and choices was endless, but the goal was always the same. Each surface of the cube had to be uniform in colour. God doesn't seem to me to have designed the kind of game where you must have a matching set of coloured squares on each face of the cube to have got it right. He appears to enjoy the full spectrum of colours and possibilities blended together. At times they complement one another and on other occasions they contrast, just like the endless variety in creation. Even grass is not a standard green; it has a multiplicity of shades which themselves change with the seasons. While we enjoy this riot of colour and diversity, let us not turn the church into a Rubik Cube, with one predictable outcome. A multi-coloured, ever-changing rainbow is much more in tune with God's design.

I don't know whether you realise it, but even the ordinary Rubik Cube is quite amazing. Every time you twist the squares, even without any effort or great concentration, the new pattern you have formed is unique. There are millions of alternatives and each one is as rare and unusual as the uniform one most people are seeking to make. So it is with each one of us and the ways in which we can come together to give glory to God. No two Christians are the same and no combination of lives will ever achieve the same pattern. In the spiritual realm the potential is even greater than in the physical world. Our creative God places his infinite and eternal life in each one who comes to him. We shall never run out of ways to satisfy his heart, or to please one another. That's why we need eternity to try. Please, my brothers and sisters, I beg you, start right now to utilise all the shades and colours Jesus has placed within you, so that he might see all the fullness of his coming kingdom displayed through his people here on earth before he comes again. We do well to read Ephesians 3:8–10 this way:

> ...this grace was given to preach the unsearchable riches of Christ, and to make all people see what is the plan of the mystery hidden for ages in God who created all things; that through the church the rainbow-coloured wisdom of God might now be made known.